Trusting Me, Trusting You

INTERPERSONAL COMMUNICATION SERIES

Bobby R. Patton and Kim Giffin, Editors

Trusting Me, Trusting You

Kim Giffin
The University of Kansas

Richard E. Barnes
University of Wisconsin-Milwaukee

Charles E. Merrill Publishing Company
A Bell & Howell Company
Columbus, Ohio

Published by
Charles E. Merrill Publishing Company
A Bell & Howell Company
Columbus, Ohio 43216

This book was set in Helios.
The Production Editors were Beverly Kolz and Lynn Walcoff.
The cover was designed by Will Chenoweth.

Library of Congress Catalog Card Number: 75-26283

International Standard Book Number: 0-675-08647-7

Photo on p. 2 by Editorial Photocolor Archives/Doug Magee; Photo on p. 40 by Editorial Photocolor Archives/Andrew Sacks.
All other photos by Hank Young.
Cartoons by Robert Galeotti, unless otherwise credited.

1 2 3 4 5 6—80 79 78 77 76

Printed in the United States of America

Contents

Foreword

Most people today want closer ties with other people. This desire can be found in all walks of life as more and more people are attempting to share feelings as well as ideas and opinions. The other person is being viewed as someone with the right to be heard and his/her feelings considered, rather than just an object to be noted or manipulated.

This yearning for closer personal relationships as well as an awareness of the needs of others has developed as a response to the heightened state of impersonal attitudes, individual isolation, and job insulation of our increasingly automated and complex society.

The way we interact is viewed as the key to meeting this need. We are becoming more aware of the value of interpersonal communication as a process. More and more people are coming to perceive others with whom they are in daily contact—other workers on the job, other students in classes—as potential personal friends rather than just associates. The desired goal of reaching out and touching the lives of other people and having their lives touch us rests upon our ability to use the process of interpersonal communication.

The academic study of interpersonal communication is truly interdisciplinary. Scholars from such fields as psychology, sociology, linguistics, business, education, and speech communication have examined human behavior and attempted to formulate theories of human interaction. During the last decade the curricula of many disciplines have been expanded to include a variety of courses focused upon the process of interpersonal communication.

This series was conceived from a felt need to supply concise, readable instructional materials that reflect sound scholarship and direct relevancy for the reader. Whether a single book is used for a unit in a course or several books are used to form a total course, we believe that the books in this series will prove practical. We think that any reader interested in improving his/her interpersonal communication will profit from reading these books.

In the eight books of this series an effort has been made to supply practical applications of theory to our lives. Some of the books deal with certain situational applications of interpersonal communication, such as between persons of different races, between intimate partners, between working colleagues, between associates in a classroom or as members of a small group. The other books deal with selected important parts of the interpersonal process itself such as learning to trust one another, becoming more open and frank and utilizing our nonverbal communication skills. Each of the authors has a record of scholarship and experience that uniquely equips him/her to write in that special area. We believe that each book in the series is a valuable contribution to the literature on interpersonal communication.

We thank the authors for their efforts and the cooperation that has made this series possible. In addition we would like to acknowledge the contribution and strong support provided by our editor, Tom Hutchinson, and his associates Beverly Kolz and Lynn Walcoff. We hope that our combined efforts have made this book of personal value to you.

Bobby R. Patton

Kim Giffin

Preface

Most books about communication between people provide a broad overview of the symbolic act. They provide a smorgasbord of theory and research covering such diverse topics as semantics, group behavior, listening, source credibility, and so forth. These broad treatments of communication are generally written as texts for introductory courses. While we have no complaint with this approach for general purposes, it does seem to us that a brief, succinct treatment of the most important communication behaviors is necessary. We are increasingly being called upon by people in and out of the academic community to explain central ideas necessary for improved communication behaviors.

The manager of an industrial plant wants to know what he can do to improve his relations with his employees. Principals ask how they can improve their rapport with teachers; and teachers, in turn, ask how they can assure a supportive climate in the classroom. Families and couples increasingly seek professional assistance for overcoming their "communication breakdowns."

This book does not purport to provide an answer to all the problems related to communication. It does address what we believe is a central concept for most person-to-person communication. In order for effective communication to develop, *trust* is absolutely necessary. No matter what type of communication is being practiced, the foundation of the prescriptive literature advocates trust. Ancient Greek rhetoricians advocated that speakers must develop ethos with the audience. More contemporary speech communication scholars have referred to the necessity for credibility. Small group practitioners and human relations scholars have advocated developing a climate of psychological safety or support. Educators have long recognized that effective teaching is dependent upon rapport. All these terms and concepts have one common characteristic—trust. For this reason, we believe that the student and practitioner of communication should be provided a brief prescriptive treatment of the topic.

The organization of the chapters is based upon our definition of trust. Chapter 1 is an overview of the nature of trust and introduces some fundamental communication terminology. Chapter 2 discusses self trust as a necessary prerequisite to communicating with others. Chapter 3 argues that a person must trust him/herself in order to recognize potential worth in others. Chapter 4 turns the issue around by maintaining that trust of others is necessary for development of self. Chapter 5 describes those factors we perceive in others that lead us to trust them. Chapters 6 and 7 explore issues of risk and ethics. In general, we argue that trust has desirable effects for all participants in communication transactions.

We wish to express our gratitude to the many significant others who provided the impetus for this project and to our children at home: Charlie and Kitty Giffin and Stacy and Shaun Barnes who provided enjoyable diversions from the task. Finally, to Charlene and Roanne who gave the project special meaning.

Trusting Me, Trusting You

Trust:

A Communication Construct

Did you ever have to stand at your desk in grade school and multiply numbers as the teacher pointed to different combinations on the board? Or did you ever have to stand and read a passage from a poem or short story? For some students the opportunity to perform in front of classmates is rewarding. Remember the glow of satisfaction gained from having whizzed through the "nine times" table without any errors? The teacher probably rewarded the behavior with a "very good" comment and you may have envisioned each of the classmates eyeing you enviously. For others, the experience may have been more traumatic. You may have worked on the multiplication table at home the night before but when the teacher called upon you to stand, your knees felt weak and a lump came to your throat as the teacher pointed to the "eight times" table. Somehow all the previous study seemed to flee to the playground as you stumbled on 8 times 4. By the time you missed two more combinations the teacher asked you to take your seat and another student was called upon. Humiliation burned as you felt the eyes of the class upon you and imagined each of your friends snickering behind your back.

For most of us, grade school was probably a combination of successes and failures. Failure and humiliation from a multiplication table was compensated with success in foot races across the playground. A stumbling, faulty reading ability was at least partially compensated by a drawing of an elephant placed on display. But it is safe to suggest that we all watched for *feedback* from others.

PERCEPTION OF FEEDBACK

Much of our behavior is a conscious, or perhaps unconscious, desire to gain a response from others. Feedback can be regarded as a response to our behavior.[1] Common examples of *nonverbal feedback* include a smile, a hit, or merely a momentary focus of attention. (Nonverbal feedback is regarded as all nonlinguistic or extralinguistic aspects of behavior that have meaning for us.) *Verbal feedback* can take the form of a lengthy lecture, a simple sentence of praise or blame, or even a passing word of recognition such as "hi." Whatever form feedback takes, the sender of the original behavior is acknowledged and fed information as a means of controlling future behavior. If a hitchhiker is quickly successful in obtaining a ride, the means used, such as looking the passing motorist in the eye and appearing concerned, are reinforced to the extent that the hitchhiker will probably use the same behavior the next time he/she needs a ride. Furthermore, unless subsequent actions on the part of the driver interfere, the entire act of hitchhiking is reinforced. Thus, perhaps inadvertently, the driver has perpetuated the original behavior. If, on the other hand, the driver chose to acknowledge the presence of the hitchhiker and passed on by or stopped for the hitchhiker but proceeded to verbally or physically attack the rider, the original behavior would be weakened.

A popular anecdote concerns a debate between a famous behaviorist and a well-known advocate of psychotherapy. According to the story, the debate took place in an auditorium filled with stu-

Feedback comes in all forms.

dents and faculty at a major California university. The psychotherapist presented his arguments first. Basically, he maintained that people are not mere respondents to outside stimuli but instead are free to choose their behavior. Upon completion of his remarks, he took a seat while the behaviorist moved to the microphone. The behaviorist turned to the psychotherapist and said, "Now let me see if I understand your position. You believe that people are free to choose their behavior and are not conditioned by their environment?" "That is correct," replied the psychotherapist. "All right then, roll the tape." A large screen was lowered from the ceiling at the front of the auditorium and a videotape was run showing the psychotherapist delivering his earlier remarks. The behaviorist pointed out that the therapist was obviously right-handed since most of his gestures for emphasis were made with his right hand. The camera panned to the front, center section of the auditorium where a large segment of students were showing varying degrees of disapproval by nodding their heads back and forth, frowning, and providing other nonverbal responses to the speaker. The behaviorist explained that these students were confederates engaged in a little experiment. As the videotape continued to play, the students were shown smiling and nodding

approval each time the speaker used his left hand. By the end of the tape, the psychotherapist was shown lecturing with his right hand in his pocket and gesturing entirely with his left hand. The behaviorist rested his case by noting that the students had been able to effectively alter the behavior of the psychotherapist by providing nonverbal cues which were perceived as rewarding and punishing.

The humor of this anecdote is, of course, based upon the psychotherapist's being unaware that his behavior was being modified by planned feedback. Conversely, many times we are unaware of the effect of our response upon others. Parents of young children sometimes seek to provide comfort to a child who awakens in the night by taking the child into the warmth of their own bed. Unfortunately, after just a few trips to the parent's bed the child "learns" to cry every night since the behavior is rewarded by the parental touch and warmth. Parents become frustrated as the undesired behavior of the child becomes more frequent. They are often unaware that their own behavior is rewarding the crying of the child.

In much the same way, all our communication is a means of gaining a response and having an effect. A response is made intentionally or unintentionally to acknowledge reception of the verbal behavior and to control future behavior.

Emergence of Self from Feedback

As existing psycho-physical beings, we act as stimuli in search of responses. During the early years of childhood we seek an identity by means of feedback. Developmental psychologists vary in their estimates of the formative years, but generally the most significant period is placed between the ages of two and seven.[2] The feedback received during the formative years from siblings, parents, and other significant persons with whom we were in regular contact, and whose responses we value, served to shape our self-perception. Whether we like ourselves or not, who we are today is probably a reflection of how we perceived others responding to us at a much earlier stage in our lives. There is some evidence to suggest that our self-concept is moderately stable by the ninth grade.[3] That is, we will have gained a fairly good conception of who we are in relation to others and become less susceptible to change in response to feedback from others.

Before you slide on by what we have just said, you might want to reflect on whether you agree with the theory, because the idea of our self-concept being gained from others is not totally accepted. College freshmen enamored with the joy of freedom from the bonds of parents often are reluctant to agree that they may be extensions of their parents. Fired with the spirit of independence, adolescents somehow believe that they will be significantly different (better) than their parents. Often by the time the person reaches his/her late twenties he/she begins to recognize that both good and bad traits identified in the parents are found in his/her self. Harris and others in transactional analysis explain that each of us records in his/her memory the thoughts, feelings, and actions of his/her early childhood experiences.[4] This memory tape is available for replaying at any time, given the proper stimulus.

From a positive perspective, because your parents repeatedly told you to look both ways before entering the street as a child, in later years you stop and look for traffic before retrieving your own child's ball. The same memory tape can potentially result in dysfunctional behavior. If, for example, you heard your father verbally abuse your mother for failing to have his shirts ironed, as a husband you may respond in exactly the same manner to a similar situation without taking into account the inappropriateness of your father's original act, that your wife has a full-time job outside the home, and that our cultural norms have changed in regard to role expectations.

When one of the writers of this book went to pick up his children at a friend's house he observed the friend's daughter run outside in the cold damp weather without any shoes. "Sophie," he yelled, "get some shoes on or you will catch cold." When the girl ignored the parental plea he called to the mother, "Sophie is outside without any shoes." The mother's response, "She will come in when she gets chilly," was completely unexpected. Perhaps Sophie's mother had thought through the issue of clothing for her child and knew that physicians now admit that the common cold disease is not caused by chilly temperatures, or perhaps the mother's parental tape simply didn't conform to the common superstition about the source of colds. Without asking we can't know the source of the response. But we do know that the original admonition came from playing a parent memory tape rather than thinking through the issue. The author of this book was saying and doing exactly the same thing his parents said and did when he was a child.

An important qualification for this theory of children becoming extensions of their parents is that a rebellious trait, fostered by significant others, may result in the young adult developing in the opposite direction of his parents. In either case, who we are as persons is gained in large part by perceived feedback and responses.

INTRA AND INTERPERSONAL COMMUNICATION

This awareness of self is gained primarily by means of *intra* and *interpersonal communication*. Intrapersonal communication refers to the dialogue a person conducts with him/herself. We behave in a certain manner and then, through our own perceptions of ourselves, feed back this information to our central nervous system as a means of controlling future behavior. If a person attempts to ski and after several rather ungraceful falls concludes that he/she is just too uncoor-

dinated to ski, he/she will probably not venture out onto the slopes again because of intrapersonal communication about the perceived lack of coordination. Someone more experienced in skiing might be able to detect fundamental mistakes that could be overcome with practice. Thus, a potential second source of information about ourselves is derived from others' communication. We selectively perceive certain cues from others to serve as feedback for controlling future behavior. The meaning of the feedback may vary immensely from person to person particularly in the case of nonverbal cues. Upon introducing him/herself to another person, the insecure person may feel embarrassed when his/her remarks are met with laughter. A socially secure person may perceive the laughter as a positive response to a charismatic personality, while a third person may regard the laughter as the response of a social process occurred between two or more people that we will call interpersonal communication. When a person responds to a meaningful stimulus, communication has occurred.

A Receiver Orientation

A key consideration in this rather broad definition of communication is the idea that meaning is imparted by the receiver rather than the sender of a message.[5] If a stimulus is not perceived or has no meaning for the receiver, then communication has not occurred. Recently when swimming in a nearby pool a group of swimmers started shouting gibberish to the extent that the walls reverberated with sound. The vocalizations could be heard by anyone present but unless a person was one of the "in" group, the shouting only consisted of noise without meaning. Communication from some receivers' points of view had not occurred. In a similar manner, if you were accidentally to enroll in an advanced chemistry course before having taken the introductory course, the instructor might not "communicate" with you because of your lack of meanings for the concepts and terminology being discussed. Clearly a message is sent but lack of past experience to provide meaning for the message may result in a lack of communication.

A receiver orientation to communication is a particularly important concept in the development of self. To follow our reasoning, you must begin with the premise that the meaning of a communication is not externally located in reality but instead is formulated in the mind of the receiver. Naturally, as senders of a message we try to make ourselves "perfectly clear" (in the words of a former president). In order to achieve clarity, we try to select words that accurately reflect our

perception of reality. The problem is that we can rarely see reality in exactly the same way as all our receivers, and the language we select to reflect our perceptions may "mean" something entirely different to others.[6] Former President Nixon serves as an example of a person who tried to select language carefully in order to achieve clarity, but whose auditors constantly perceived the message from a different perspective.

"LET ME MAKE THIS PERFECTLY CLEAR!!!"

A consultant to business and industry indicates that one of the most prevalent communication problems of managers is the assumption that once they have said something, it will be understood by others in the same manner.[7] What constitutes a recession, a good-looking guy, a fink, and so on? Each of us uses his/her own criteria. Therefore, the picture that is brought to mind and acted upon by the receiver may be much different from the one intended by the sender. In return, feedback perceived by the sender as encouraging of behavior may not have been intended to be encouraging. For example, a female smiling at a strange male in this country is generally regarded as friendly, but in some foreign nations the smile may be much more linked to sexual connotations.

In the same vein, our behavior may be congruent with how we *perceive* others viewing us but may be unrelated to how others *actually* view us. A study of college females' perception of how they perceived their parents' viewing them demonstrated that the college girls behaved in accordance with how they *thought* their parents viewed them.[8] A later study asked ninth-grade students how they perceived their parents' view of themselves, and once again the students were found to behave in the manner they perceived their parents' evaluation of them. This time, however, the researchers carried the investigation one step further and asked the parents how they *actually* viewed their children. The results indicated that how parents actually perceive children is not correlated with how children perceive their parents view them.[9] Therefore, in terms of the developmental behavior of the child, the feedback the parents thought they were providing the child was not as directly related to the child's behavior as was the child's perception of feedback from parents.

Self-Fulfilling Prophecy

At this point we have suggested that a sense of self develops from perceived feedback from others. Actual feedback from others may not be as important to self-development as the meaning attributed to selected feedback from others. This may sound somewhat like a self defining self and to some extent that conclusion is true. Each person tends to operate on the basis of a *self-fulfilling prophecy*. A self-concept is developed, and thereafter the person selects and shapes information to fit the previously held convictions. The salesman who has no faith in himself or his product asks the customer, "You wouldn't want to buy this, would you?" Sure enough, after having been turned down several times he concludes, "I knew I couldn't sell that product." The salesman communicated with others in a subconscious style designed to fulfill the previously held conviction regarding his sales ability.

We communicate in order to check out our perception of reality. Through our selection of language we recommend to others that they perceive reality the way we perceive it. When you exclaim to your friend, "That is a great movie!" you are not only implicitly recommending that your friend attend the showing but also that he/she evaluate it positively. Our view of reality is in part determined by the feedback from others which is filtered in terms of our preconceived notion of reality. To extend the example of the movie a bit further, when a critical review of the film appears in the newspaper, we tend to focus upon portions confirming our previously held convictions as support for our evaluation and tend to discount, or argue with, those portions which suggest a contrary evaluation. Each of us develops a mental network, or constructs, based upon past experiences as a means of viewing the present reality and anticipating the future.[10] In the early years of development the child learns to construe reality in a particular way. When later

experience fails to confirm these constructions, some alteration is made in the mental network. Thus, we are constantly undergoing mental change in order to provide a better fit with reality.[11]

As a consequence, our conception of ourselves is constantly undergoing change as we perceive feedback from others failing to fit our previously held anticipations of behavior from others. A limitation to this principle is that each of us has a personality core, or belief system, which is resistant to change. Nonconfirming feedback from others is dealt with mentally in such a way as to assure a fit with previously held convictions. In a study conducted by Eagly, students were provided negative feedback.[12] The results indicated that when low self-esteem persons perceive negative feedback from others they are more likely to change their attitude toward self in a negative direction than will high self-esteem persons. Those with high self-esteem resisted change in the negative direction and even used the information to change self-concept in a favorable direction. This book focuses upon the perceptual process by which we learn to trust our intrapersonal communication (self-reliance), and we learn to trust our interpersonal communication (reliance on others) as a means of developing greater awareness of self and our potentialities.

TRUST DEFINED

Trust refers to person P who relies upon person O in a risk-taking situation in order to achieve an uncertain objective.[13] The symbol O refers to the perceived person (or behavior) and P refers to the perceiver.[14]

Intrapersonal Trust

In the case of *intrapersonal trust* P and O refer to the same person. We anticipate our behavior (O) to produce a certain effect. Upon selectively observing the behavior, we mentally apply meaning to it as the proximal stimulus (P), thus communicating with ourselves. Numerous writers and speakers have urged people to develop a positive view of their potential, or in other words, to develop intrapersonal trust.[15] An athlete is capable of accomplishing only that which he/she believes possible. If the high jumper does not believe that he/she is capable of clearing seven feet, then the chances are dim that the feat will be achieved. You undoubtedly will remember the children's story of the little engine that could. When faced with a steep hill to climb, the engine puffed, "I think I can, I think I can," and when the crest was mounted, the engine happily puffed, "I

THERE ARE:

THOSE WHO SAY I CAN'T

THOSE WHO SAY I CAN

THEY ARE BOTH RIGHT

knew I could, I knew I could." In terms of the definition of trust: O is the expectation of behavior (the anticipated ability, or lack of ability, to climb the hill); P is the selected perception of accomplishment (observation of progress up the hill); risk involves potential loss of physical and psychological well being (if the engine fails, will he ever be able to climb any other hill?); and the uncertain objective involves the issue of risking potential defeat from the outset (if the engine does not attempt to mount the hill no one will blame him because of his size, but if he does attempt the climb, the objective is probably grounded in some unclearly defined psychological need for self-esteem). Thus, in intrapersonal trust one person relies upon him/herself to accomplish a psychological goal in a situation where the potential loss is greater than the gain. Upon assessment of the effect a mental adjustment is made, if necessary, to better anticipate future behaviors.

Interpersonal Trust

Interpersonal trust involves two people. O responds to the presence and/or behavior of P, and P in turn selectively perceives the feedback of O. Both persons' future behavior is contingent upon the perceived meaning of feedback from the other. In this case, trust refers to the reliance upon the communication of the other fitting the previously held anticipation of effects. Since both persons are simultaneously exchanging information by responding to the other, concepts such as "sender" and "receiver" become meaningless in terms of the on-going nature of process. Information theorist Wilber Schramm has applied the useful concept of coupling to interpersonal com-

munication.[16] He suggests that when two people become linked together in their psychological space there is an information exchange which can be regarded as communication.

RISK

Applying Schramm's conceptualization to our definition of trust, P and O are coupled together in a situational environment of time and space.[17] Inherent in this link is the element of risk. Each person exposes self to another with the concurrent risk of perceiving feedback from the other incongruent with currently held predictions or expectations. The amount of risk is determined by the ratio of potential loss to gain. In a low risk condition, the potential gain for the individual will exceed the perceived potential loss. Conversely, high risk involves a perceived potential loss exceeding gain. Trust is said to be directly correlated with amount of risk involved. The greater the risk, the greater the potential trust. When an Army platoon leader orders his men to jump out of their foxholes and to charge toward the enemy, great physical risk is involved. Therefore, when the men obey, they are said to have placed high trust in their leader. Less apparent, but no less real, is the psychological risk we take in communicating with others. When a student makes a statement in class, there is a risk of negatively perceived feedback from the instructor and fellow class members.

Again, it is important to remember that communication occurs in the mind of the perceiver. The risk involved in an interpersonal context is unique to each individual. For some individuals there may be little risk in making a contribution to class discussion, but for others even saying one's own name may be fear arousing with threat potential. The risk involved is represented by how the individual anticipates the situational effects rather than how any "outside," objective observer would view the situation.

Uncertain Objective

In the case of the soldier charging the enemy position, the ultimate objective of defeating the enemy may be relatively clear. But why should an individual soldier rely upon the directive of his commanding officer? For the good of the unit? In order to establish credibility with the officer and the other members of the platoon? Or because hesitancy could result in harm to himself and to others? Whatever the reason, the soldier probably would not be able to explain why he relied upon (trusted) the officer at that precise moment.

The uncertainty of the objective is even more apparent in the case of the student participating in a class discussion. Few instructors use class participation as the sole criterion for grades so there are small demand characteristics in that regard. Why venture an opinion in the class? Certainly there is risk involving loss of esteem, but what can be gained? Improved self-esteem? Increased credibility with the instructor? Perhaps a more meaningful discussion? All of these may be factors, but an individual would probably be hard put to respond to the question of why the risk was taken.

Throughout the following chapters we will be referring to trust as P relying on O in order to achieve an uncertain objective in a risky situation. Naturally, not all theorists define trust in the same way. When studies are cited which treat trust from alternative perspectives, we will identify the differences.

TRUST PRESCRIBED

Before going any further we will state unabashedly that this book is prescriptive as well as descriptive. Historically the speech communication discipline has been devoted to the improvement of communication skills. Trust has implicitly been the focus of scholars dating back to ancient Greece. Aristotle, in presenting his tripartite plan of proofs, explained ethos as a technique used to persuade audiences.[18] A successful speaker must be perceived as exhibiting qualities of honesty, sound judgment, and an interest in the welfare of the listeners, according to Aristotle, in order to induce the audience to give a fair hearing to the arguments. Ancient Greeks were primarily concerned with the establishment of trust from a "sender" view. The ethos of Aristotle refers to trust of a speaker by an audience and is similar to the concept of source credibility coined two thousand years later by three social psychologists.[19]

From the opposite perspective, a communicator (sender) is risking self in terms of responses of his/her listeners. The reliance of a speaker upon a listener has been referred to as psychological safety[20] and supportive climate.[21] Both concepts refer to a situational atmosphere conducive to increasing the speaker's confidence. Rogers' psychological safety is achieved by having a listener exhibit high degrees of accurate empathy, warmth, and genuineness. The supportive climate advocated by Gibb may be achieved when a respondent utilizes several interpersonal communication behaviors including spontaneity, empathy, equality, provisionalism, description, and problem orientation.

From either the speaker or respondent perspective, scholars have advocated trust as a means of increasing communicative effectiveness. We are of the same mind. After having researched the construct from its earliest form to its latest advocates, after having conducted many groups of students who profess to have low trust of their own and others' communicative behaviors, we are more convinced than ever that the central construct for good interpersonal relations is trust.

ETHICS

The final chapter of the book is devoted to the difficult issue of ethics in communication. There can be no question that a portion of alienation and loneliness commonly identified with twentieth-century man[22] is due to withdrawal from atrocities committed by our fellow man. The withdrawn, distrustful individual many times has reason to be cynical. Too often when a person risks his/her psycho-physical self in trusting others, he/she is stripped of his/her being and raped in front of a perceived uncaring society. The scared person many times has learned to hide skillfully behind contrived roles and has functioned in a game-like manner only to discover that he/she has lost sight of his/her own identity and any meaningful relationship with others.

As respondents and controllers of others' communication, we have an obligation to the other person to honor the trust placed in us. Each time we fail to uphold the trusting relationship we increase the danger of doing permanent damage to the relationship and to the other person. Furthermore, we demonstrate to ourselves our incapacity to sustain a meaningful, positive relationship. The crooked politician who steps on others as he climbs the political stairs and the shyster investment broker who "rips off" his/her friends, has each used communicative skills to gain the trust of others. But based upon the concept of feedback from others, each time a relationship ends in disaster, a portion of the individual dies.

SUMMARY

In this chapter we have tried to provide you with an overview of the remaining chapters. We have defined trust as person P (the perceiver) relying upon person O (the observed) in a risk-taking situation in order to achieve an uncertain objective. Trust in one's self has been discussed in terms of intrapersonal communication and trust in others pertains to interpersonal communication. In either case, trust is realized from an individual perception of behavioral effects and may or may not reflect other individuals' perceptions of the same effects. Therefore, throughout the book we will be regarding trust as an individual's unique perception of reality as distinguished from some external conception of "truth."

Chapter 2 will explore the issue of a person's reliance upon self.

2

Self-trust as a Benefit to Self

Basic to a conception of trust is a realization of self. A person's perception of others is colored by the person's perception of self. While it is true that a person's self-concept is shaped by others, it is also true that a sense of self is gained through an inner dialogue, or intrapersonal communication. This chapter will focus upon the trust of one's self as a benefit to self. The reader should keep in mind, however, that self-concept is gained through both intra and interpersonal communication.

SELF-CONCEPT

Self-concept refers to a person's introspective view of his/her physical appearance, feelings, attitudes, personality, and values. If you were to ask the question "Who am I?" the words, phrases and explanations with which you would answer constitute your self-concept. Some of the words might be obvious objective terms like male and black, while other terms might be subjective and known only to yourself such as shy, concerned-for-others, and short. The idea of self-concept is not that others see you as short, for example, but that you see yourself as short. All of us would probably include words and phrases on the list that others would be surprised to read. Furthermore, we probably add value judgments to the conceptions of self that others would not value in the same way. In one of our classes there was an attractive coed who revealed that she was going to undergo a painful operation for removal of freckles from her arms and face. The idea of removing her freckles was dismaying to some of the male members of the class because, in their opinion, part of the coed's attractiveness was her freckles. Yet, considering the expense and discomfort she was willing to accept, she must have placed a much different value on the freckles than the males' perception of them.

It may be safe to suggest that all of us have physical appearances that we negatively value and seek to remedy. Heavy people seek to reduce, thin people seek to gain weight, short people wear shoes with platforms, and tall people wear flat-heeled shoes. At the same time, all these terms are relative to the individual. What constitutes heavy, thin, short, and tall? Except in extreme cases, the terms are probably mere subjective value judgments.

The subjectiveness of self-perceptions becomes even more individualized when psychological traits are added. Personality theorists indicate that we all have every possible personality dimension in our psychological make-up.[1] The following list of words shows traits identified by some of our students as representative of themselves and others. How many of the traits would you apply to yourself? Would you admit that at one time or another you have exhibited each of the traits? What distinguishes one person from another is generally not the presence or absence of a particular trait but rather the degree of the trait. For example, a friendly person is simply more friendly than a person regarded as unfriendly. Therefore, the friendly person may not see him/herself as any friendlier than the unfriendly person sees him/herself.

TABLE 1. 25 Self-concept traits generated by college students

worldly	religious	dependent	swinger	prejudiced
broad intellect	young	inconsiderate	rigid	predictable
daring	likes sweets	sexy	envious	opinionated
honest	bitchy	friendly	close	lazy
normal	excitable	rugged	gullible	mature

Palm readers, astrologers, and soothsayers sometimes take advantage of this fact by telling clients about personality traits found in all of us. In talking with students, we occasionally illustrate the point by asking for a volunteer to let us identify his/her personality traits based upon his/her physical appearance.[2] The volunteer is asked to face the audience and nod agreement or disagreement as we stand behind the person attempting to identify his/her traits. We reveal to the audience a pre-typed description to demonstrate that there is nothing in the person's actual appearance that has permitted the personality depiction. All items are worded to sound appropriate to the individual. An item such as "the person is generally easy going but is at times rather emotional" is characteristic of everyone, but each person tends to see the trait as unique to him/herself. As we proceed the person nods agreement to each correct item and disagreement to each incorrect item. Invariably the person agrees with a large majority of the items and is amazed by our insight and expertise. We then reveal to the person that we were not basing our personality profile on his/her appearance, but instead we were reading a predetermined series of traits.

Most con artists, of course, do not reveal that their information is not prepared specifically for the individual. One of our students worked for a state fair carnival vendor who operates a computerized hand writing analysis. Part of the publicity includes a money back guarantee if the analysis is incorrect. According to the student, a large number of people are always willing to plunk down fifty cents and rarely does anyone ask for a refund. One of four basic output messages is printed regardless of how an individual signs an input computer card. If you were to invest in the analysis, the chances are about one in four that you would get the following message:

> You enjoy privacy and do not care for insincere admiration
> You have a reckless side to your outwardly solid nature
> You are generous and enjoy giving to others
> You live by your high principles
> You are a seeker of facts and cannot be easily fooled

Would you ask for a refund? Probably not, because you can see yourself in the personality profile. We should add that there is a legitimate study of hand writing that could be programmed into a computer. For all we know there may be varying degrees of legitimate computer hand writing analyses available to the public. We will leave that issue to your own conclusion. Our point is that all generalized personality profiles are accurate to the extent that all of us share varying degrees of the same traits.

SELF-ACCEPTANCE

In general, the physical and psychological traits we ascribe to ourselves are not unique to us as individuals, but the values and dimensions attributed to the traits are unique to each of us. Some of the traits will be positively valued while others are negatively valued.

An article which recently appeared in a newspaper discussed the problem of identifying "gifted" children.[3] Psychologists have operationalized the trait of "gifted" by administering a series of tests to children to determine whether the child is significantly above average in abstract thinking, dexterity, and so forth. Part of the problem is that intelligence is a relative concept. All children are to some degree intelligent and the parent may have difficulty knowing when the child is significantly different from other children. The problem is compounded by the value parents attach to intelligence. Some parents are embarrassed about having a gifted child. As one parent explained, she would be pleased if her son was a superior athlete but she is somewhat embarrassed about her gifted son's academic prowess. In this case, the parent is placing a positive value on athletic ability and a negative value on scholarship, or at least perceives society as embracing these value judgments.

If we were to sum across all the trait values, taking into consideration the saliency or importance the trait holds for an individual, an eventual degree of positive or negative self-concept could be established. Negative self-concept may be somewhat of a misnomer since no "normal" individual may dislike him/herself. Consistency theorists have suggested that since we are positively attached to ourselves, we must to some degree like ourselves.[4] The general value of our self-image should be thought of in terms of a

The real and ideal selves.

continuum of positive judgments from strong self-acceptance to weak self-acceptance.

At least two other views of self-concept exist. One is the self that we perceive others as perceiving. This conception of self will be dealt with in chapter 4. The other is the self that we view as ideal. The ideal self-image is characterized as containing elements of early childhood wishes for power and knowledge.[5] During the developmental process there is a gradual modification of overidealizations in terms of more realistic and reasonable goals and values. The ideal self-image includes concepts internalized from the culture, family, and peers. For example, try to imagine the traits of a person whom you admire and seek to emulate. The person may not be perfect in the sense that all traits could be identified on some objective basis as beyond reproach but rather the traits probably reflect characteristics which are salient to you. Tough-minded might not seem to be a desirable trait to some of us but for wishy-washy Charlie Brown the trait might be perceived as highly desirable. Some, or all, of the dominant traits that you perceive in the admired person may be characteristic traits of your ideal self.

Another way to determine your ideal self is to write a single word on a note card describing a personality or physiological trait of a person, e.g., fat, friendly, cool, conceited. Do this for as many traits as you can think of, using one card per word. When you have completed the task, place the stack of cards in front of you and sort out all traits which you regard as desirable or ideal. Upon completion, record on a sheet of paper all the ideal traits. This list of traits can be re-

garded as your ideal self. Next, place all the trait cards together and again proceed through the stack, this time identifying the traits most like your "real" self. This total card-shuffling procedure is referred to by researchers as a Q-sort technique.

The amount of agreement between ideal self and real self is indicative of the amount of your self-acceptance, or self-esteem.[6] A large discrepancy between the two sets of traits is indicative of a relatively low degree of self-acceptance; a marked similarity between the two sets of traits may reflect higher self-acceptance, or in other words, intrapersonal trust. The Q-sort procedure permits a person to identify traits of a desired self and a real self using terms unique to the individual as a means of identifying the degree of self-acceptance. It is possible for traits selected as real and ideal to be negatively valued by society, yet if the two sets are similar an individual could still exhibit high self-acceptance/ intrapersonal trust. A good example of a negatively defined trait from a societal perspective, but ideal and real for the individual, is "bank robber" as perceived by Clyde Barrow, depicted in the movie *Bonnie and Clyde*. Even though bank robbing and killing are not positively valued in a society of law, Clyde was proud of his accomplishments. You may recall that Bonnie even wrote a poem glorifying the Barrow gang and they took a picture of themselves for the newspapers. In a far less dramatic fashion but equally relevant manner, a person might view him/herself as cold and calculating and place a positive value on the traits in terms of an ideal self in spite of the fact that most people value the personality traits of warmth and spontaneity.

Implicit Personality

Most of us, however, do not sit down and systematically determine our self-concept. Instead, we tend to operate on an implicit system of which we may be only vaguely aware. While a person may not be consciously aware of his/her self-perceived body image, he/she will make decisions based upon implicit assumptions about him/her self. For example, in selecting a bathing suit, a brief, tight-fitting style may be selected in preference to a more modest style by a person with a positive body image. Another person, in contrast, may rationalize that the weather is too cold or too hot for swimming as a means of coping with a negatively perceived body image. This implicit system of self-assumptions is constantly being modified based upon experiences, but in general is relatively stable over time particularly for those with positive self-images.

The idea that a person has an implicit perception of self in relation to others helps explain the regularities of behavior. Do you characteristically initiate conversations with strangers? Do you regularly volunteer opinions and information in groups? Your answer to these questions is largely determined by the conclusions you have drawn from past experiences. However, most of us don't stop to process why we habitually behave the way we do, nor do we generally even consider alternative forms of behavior. We recently asked for three volunteers out of a group of ninety adults. Each of the three people who volunteered was physiologically attractive, clothing was stylish and fit nicely, and contemporary hair styles were neatly combed. In effect, our volunteers implicitly "knew" they would have a positive effect upon the audience. The comments and focus of the group reinforced the previously held assumptions which provided additional support for future volunteering.

In line with this incident, researchers have reported that individuals high in self-acceptance are more assertive, take more initiative, and defend themselves against internal and external sources of distress to a greater degree than those who express low self-acceptance.[7] In sharp contrast, a review of studies on discrepancies between real and ideal self-concept reports that persons low in self-acceptance generally are more defensive, rigid in perception, and tend to distort perceptions to a greater degree than those who indicate less discrepancy between real and ideal self.[8]

Existence Precedes Essence

Notice the circular effect of our implicit self-acceptance. The assumptions determine the acts which provide reinforcement for the assumptions. Thus, who we are is largely determined by our behavior. Philosophically speaking, our existence precedes our essence.[9] This fundamental principle of existentialism suggests that a person has no essence beyond what he/she makes of him/herself. By essence we are referring to the mental concept people have of themselves and others and by existence we mean our immediate condition of living. In other words, when we asked the question "Who Am I?" at the beginning of this chapter, the answer for each person can only be found in his/her daily act of living.

In choosing our acts, we have the freedom and responsibility of influencing our own self-image and the values attached to it. Often youth blame their parents for forcing them to behave in a particular manner or for causing them to rebel against the confines of the home. What youth are missing in both cases is that the ultimate choice of behavior as a defining act is no one else's responsibility other than their own. Youth can choose to obey or not obey, rebel or not rebel, but whatever the decision the responsibility for self-development is for the individual alone.

One of our students was complaining about an instructor who was punishing her for failing to take a mid-term and make-up exams. Clairce felt like she was being treated as a child by her instructor who was requiring her to make up the exam and docking her double for each incorrect answer. "It isn't my fault," exclaimed Clairce, "the mid-term was scheduled at the time of my favorite class in dance. I planned to come in for the make-up but my boss wouldn't let me off work." Clairce went on to explain that she tried to contact her instructor immediately after her employer told her that she would have to work. "I called Mrs. Kennedy three times between seven and eight (A.M.) but she wasn't ever in her office." As a fellow student what is your view of this case?

From our perspective Clairce had the right to choose not to take her mid-term at its regularly scheduled time. She also had the right not to take the make-up, since she probably feared loss of her job if she failed to appear. Each of those choices was hers to make. She may have felt some pressure from her dance instructor and her employer but the ultimate decision of what to do was hers alone. What she failed to consider were the possible consequences of her decisions. To avoid the weight of her responsibility, she attacked her teacher. Actually the instructor, employer, and dance teacher had little to do with influencing the choices. Since Clairce chose to attend dance class she implicitly chose to accept the responsibilities for her decisions. The dance teacher may regard her as a conscientious stu-

"Some authorities would blame your behavior on your genes, others on your home environment! . . . BUT I BLAME YOU, OTIS, plain and simple!"

Grin and Bear It *by George Lichty, Courtesy of Field Newspaper Syndicate.*

dent and the communication instructor may regard her as irresponsible. Just as the dance teacher may reward her with a solo number in the next performance, the instructor chose to punish her with a lower grade. In the process they are formulating an essence of Clairce based upon perception of her existence. The ultimate choice of her essence, however, was determined by Clairce's acts.

Many popular phrases, songs, and slogans encourage people to do their "own thing." A bumper sticker on a passing car proclaimed, "If it feels good, do it." What many proponents of "I want to be me" and "do your own thing" philosophies neglect is that with the choice of an act goes a responsibility.

If an employee wants to "tell off" his/her boss or miss work in favor of attending a political rally, that choice is rightly his/hers, but he/she must be willing to accept the consequences of being fired from the job and not receiving a favorable recommendation for future positions. The limitless freedom of choice is at the same time a boundless responsibility for what we make of ourselves.

LONELINESS

Inherent in this philosophy of self is a feeling of loneliness. We do not have a God, parent, or

enemy to blame for our failures, evil acts, or laziness, we have only ourselves to blame or praise. Therefore, in this inner dialogue with self, a person searches for the answer to "Who am I; what do I choose to do; what meaning do my acts have for me; what value do I attribute to my acts, myself, and ultimately my life?" These questions can only be answered in limited time-bound thoughts because our acts are constantly redefining the answers. If definitive answers could be found for these questions, the essence of a person could be determined.

A particularly thought-provoking scene occurs in Joseph Heller's novel *Catch-22* when the American soldiers ask the elderly Italian whom he supports in the war.[10] The old man responds, "I was a fascist when Mussolini was on top, and I am an anti-fascist now that he has been deposed. I was fanatically pro-German when the Germans were here to protect us against the Americans, and now that the Americans are here to protect us—I am fanatically pro-American." In the same way as the old man puts out his flag of allegiance on a week to week basis, we act on a day to day basis defining and redefining our existence. Only death, which ends the acts of a person, permits others to suggest answers to the essence of a person but even then definitive answers can never be known for certain since others can never know how the person perceived his/her own acts and his/her relations with the surroundings.

PAST DETERMINES PRESENT

We have referred to a person's unique capacity to develop an essence by means of existence. Another unique feature of human existence is its historicity;[11] that is, the capacity to learn from the pasts of other individuals and from one's own experiences. This concept is certainly not new to anyone. We all recognize that we learn from our parents' experiences and from our own past. The important point to consider is that the insight gained from the past serves as a screen for how we see our present condition and future acts.[12] Since no two people have exactly the same backgrounds, no one can ever fully define another's reality. Even an individual may not be fully aware of why he/she acts in a particular way until he/she introspectively explores the past. Effective person-to-person communication can help an individual to become more aware of those experiences in the past, but ultimately recognition of self must come from an introspective dialogue with self.

The idea of gaining insight into one's self based upon past experiences is an easy inferential leap to the conclusion that we act in a rational, thoughtful manner. If a person steps on the hot cement without any shoes, he/she learns quickly not to walk barefoot on the sidewalk in the middle of the summer. This type of behavior is rational and many of us pride ourselves in acting rationally based upon past experiences and anticipation of the future. William Barrett traces the development of Western culture from early Greek history and suggests that the priority Plato and Aristotle placed upon rationality and scientific thinking has resulted in a dominance of rationality for our culture, but each of us still has the option of choosing the other path for some or all of our acts.[13] In fact, the popularity of existentialism is in part traceable to the disillusionments with "a world too vast and complex to yield to human urging, and one which is indifferent—if not downright hostile—to human aspiration."[14] The act of wrinkling a computer billing card, for example, can be regarded as an irrational act in response to a cold, efficient, inhumane treatment of an individual's account. When the wrinkled statement must be hand processed rather than fed into a computer, the existence of the buyer is validated. Of course, the act carries with it the responsibility of accepting the potential cancellation of the account.

FUTURE DETERMINES PRESENT

Man/woman is not only an actor construing his/her condition based upon the past, but he/she also has the capacity to visualize and symbolize the nonexistent future. A person exists in the present and selects his/her acts by means of anticipating the effects of his/her potential acts. George Herbert Mead, the noted social psychologist, illustrated the idea in terms of boxing.[15] A boxer feints a jab in anticipation of the other boxer's response. The other boxer's anticipated counterpunch provides an opening for the significant punch by the original boxer. In the same way, a good chess player selects his/her moves on the basis of an anticipation of the countermoves by his/her opponent. In each example, the actor selects his/her behavior on the basis of a predicted future.

CONSTRUCTS

An entire system of psychotherapy has been advanced by George Kelly based upon the concept that every act of an individual makes implicit sense to that person.[16] He contends that a person construes reality based upon linguistic units

called constructs. The number, arrangement, and type of linguistic units are unique to each individual. The therapist's task is to help the client become aware of the way that reality is being construed. The behavior of the client begins to make sense when the client is aware of the way he/she is construing his/her environment and its effect upon his/her behavior. The final stage of treatment is to have the client role play another person's view of reality. Once the client is made aware of alternative perceptions he/she can choose between behaviors in anticipation of differing effects.

Usually a person seeks a therapist when he/she is psychologically uncomfortable with his/her behavioral effects upon the environment or when others are uncomfortable with the person's behavior. The construct theory of Kelly is not limited to these cases, however. According to theory, each person perceives reality on the basis of linguistic units unique to that individual. Constructs are the means by which we shape, or construe, our reality as a basis for predicting the potential effects of our behavior. If through intrapersonal communication a person can identify some of the implicit assumptions he/she is making about reality and his/her behavioral effects, then the person at least has the potential for seeing how others differ in their view of reality and the person can have greater options from which to select appropriate behavior.

In summary, an individual's self is defined by his/her behavior. The behavior is dependent upon how the individual perceives the environment as shaped by past experiences and anticipated effects of behavior. Over time, a rather stabilized view of self in relation to the environment develops from perceived patterns of rewarding or punishing experiences. The pattern and values attributed to these experiences are implicit with the individual. Through intrapersonal communication, or with the help of others, the implicit perception of reality can be made explicit. Once the individual becomes aware of the assumptions upon which he/she has been acting, the individual can choose whether he/she will continue to behave in the same manner or whether he/she will be open to alternative ways of viewing self and environment.

Ultimately the individual is alone in the choices of existence. Who he/she is, how he/she behaves, and what meaning his/her life has is dependent upon a trust of self. A negatively valued self-esteem, or low trust of self, can be correlated with certain dysfunctional behaviors while a positively valued self-esteem, high trust of self, can be correlated with behavior which tends to enhance one's relation with others.[17]

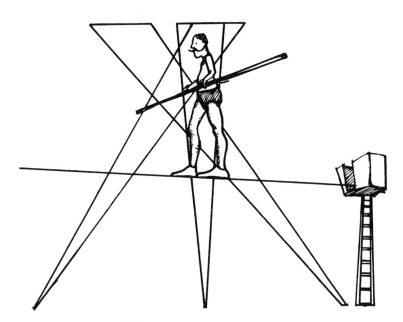

For some people, life is like walking a tightrope.

LOW SELF-TRUST

Lack of self-trust in communicating with others has been found to correlate with tendencies or impulses to over-control oneself.[18] If an individual is unsure of him/herself, he/she tends not to respond to communication opportunities but employ a wait and see attitude. The well-learned lesson is that the safest course of action is to act cautiously. Carefully controlled behavior will be reflected in a lack of initiating communication.[19]

If a person lacks trust in his/her self, the tendency is to not trust him/herself in the spotlight by introducing new ideas and behaviors to others. Jack and Lorraine Gibb report from their research that in early stages of group development members tend to view unusually restrained people as stupid, uninterested, afraid, or lazy![20] As a result, group leaders do not expect contributions from these people nor do they provide the reticent speaker with opportunities to participate. Eventually the noninitiator develops feelings of guilt and unworthiness. The guilt is due to perceived lack of contributions to the functioning of the group, and the unworthiness is associated with failure to contribute.

The combination of avoiding interactions with others, social passivity, lack of initiating capacities, resultant feelings of guilt and unworthiness, produces a sense of alienation and general anxiety. Or from the other perspective, alienation and anxiety produce the avoidance behaviors. It is empirically unethical to determine definitively which comes first in real life conditions. However, when a person lacks confidence in self, the choice of contributing or not to communica-

tion between persons is not a viable option due to the inherent risk in anticipated or perceived responses of others. At first, failure to contribute actively is more comfortable but as time passes, a self-perceived lack of contribution and involvement promotes estrangement from others. Alienation, with the attendant anxiety, forces the individual to fall back on the habitually learned safe behavior—avoidance behavior. The person withdraws from situations conducive to communication with others.[21]

SELF-FULFILLING PROPHECY

If you have followed our line of reasoning, you may have begun to notice a circularity which some theorists refer to as a self-fulfilling prophecy. Because the person with low trust of self is uncertain about his/her relations with others, he/she avoids interactions when in the presence of others. When the person is not involved in the discussion, feelings of alienation with attendant anxiety prompt withdrawal and the experience provides reinforcement for the original feeling of low trust of self. This self-fulfilling prophecy is the basis of our conclusion that the person with low trust of self has little or no viable choices in the selection of his/her behavior. With increased trust of self a person can choose to communicate or not communicate, secure in the knowledge that if the chosen behaviors have an unfavorable effect the alternatives are available.

The issue of wealth and material possessions provides an interesting analogy. It is commonly said, particularly by the upper class, that money isn't everything. The common examples of upper-class youth turning their backs on the family wealth seem to attest to the meaninglessness of material possessions. On the other hand, those with money can choose to spend, save, or give away their money, and in most cases can change their minds when the decision proves unsatisfactory. The lower-class person has no choice. He/she has little or no money to do anything beyond meeting the essentials of daily existence. Therefore, it is not the money that brings pleasure and comfort but rather the choices that are available to the wealthy person that are not available to the nonaffluent person.

In like manner, the person who has high trust of self has more options available in his/her communications with others than the person with low trust of self. The issue is not so much a question of whether a person communicates or not, but rather a question of whether a person has enough trust in self to have a viable choice of behavior. It so happens that the common choice of the self-confident communicator is to interact with others, to initiate ideas, and to behave spontaneously, much as in the case of our analogy, the wealthy generally choose to keep the money and possessions for themselves.

Since the person with self-trust has confidence in his/her relations with others, he/she initiates more and perceives rewarding experiences which reinforce the positive self-concept. In the same way that the self-fulfilling prophecy worked to the disadvantage of a person low in self-trust, the self-fulfilling prophecy works to the advantage of a person high in self-trust. Self-trust gives rise to rewarding experiences which give rise to increased self-trust. Following this reasoning, it is not surprising to learn that researchers have found that successful leaders speak favorably of themselves.[22] That is not to suggest the principle works in reverse. People with high trust of self do not always become successful leaders.

One final principle should be discussed in light of low self-trust. Some researchers have found that persons lacking confidence in communica-ting with others tend to be motivated to avoid failure.[23] The aim of the motivation to avoid failure is to minimize psychological discomfort. As we discussed earlier, the person with low self-trust avoids communication opportunities as a means of avoiding the feelings of alienation and anxiety. Persons confident in communicating with others are motivated to achieve success. Motivation to achieve success is a class of motives which may be described as appetite or approach tendencies with the aim of maximizing satisfaction.[24] In other words, the confident person seeks rewards by approaching communication opportunities, while the unsure person avoids communication opportunities as a means of avoiding punishment.

SUMMARY

Throughout this chapter we have used the terms self-trust, self-acceptance, and self-awareness almost interchangeably. We propose that the terms are separate concepts but closely related. By means of intrapersonal communication a person can become more aware of self, the implicit assumptions about self, and the environment which controls behavior. Once these assumptions are identified, the person can choose to continue to operate upon them or to select alternative assumptions. Once the person is aware of the choices and accepts the responsibility for his/her own behavior, he/she will have achieved self-acceptance. The person has accepted him/herself by owning the responsibility for his/her actions which constitute his/her being or self. Since the person is aware of him/herself and is self-accepting, the uncertainty of one's relation with reality is dissipated allowing for a sense of self-trust.

We have focused upon self-trust as a benefit to self. In the following chapter we shall discuss the benefit of trusting self as a means of perceiving potential in others.

3

Self-trust as a Seeing Potential

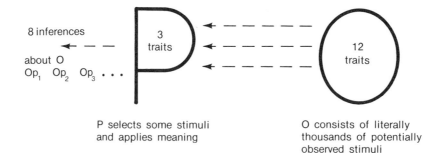

8 inferences

about O
Op_1 Op_2 Op_3 . . .

3 traits

P selects some stimuli
and applies meaning

12 traits

O consists of literally
thousands of potentially
observed stimuli

FIGURE 1

Benefit to in Others

In the previous chapter we discussed the desirability of intrapersonal trust as a benefit to self. In this chapter we will carry the concept one step further by maintaining that intrapersonal trust is a benefit to seeing potential in others—or from a negative perspective, failure to develop a positive self-acceptance will result in an inability to see others as worthy of trust. In our years of working with individuals and groups, one striking interpersonal phenomenon that seems to occur regularly is that people who are unsure of themselves are unable, or unwilling, to see potential in others.

SELECTIVE PERCEPTION

We noted in the previous chapter that each person has all personality traits to some degree. Furthermore, each person has a physical make-up and manner of behaving which communicates something of self to others. Once the person(O) is within the perceptual range of another person (P), the other person (P) will inevitably draw some tentative conclusions based upon the perceived personality, behavior, and physical traits of O. For example, O is seen sitting in the university library reading. O appears to be approximately twenty years of age, male, with moderately short hair. Some tentative inferences P might make include: (1) O is a college student, (2) studying for his classes, (3) in business administration. In reality, O might be an unemployed high school drop-out looking through the want ads for a job listing.

Part of P's error in analysis of O may be attributed to selective perception. At any one moment the sensory receptors of P can receive only limited bits of stimuli.[1] P may not have noted, for example, that O was reading a newspaper without any books, papers, and pens which commonly accompany students to the library. The selected bits of stimuli were then transmitted to the mind for screening, or mediation, and sorted according to the past experiences of P. Based upon similar bits of information from the past, P was able to make sense out of the perceived data. P is a college student so he assumes that others who use the library are also college students. Conservative appearing males that P has known were generally in business administration. Therefore, the inferences based upon selected stimuli were in large part a reflection of P rather than O. Even the initial selection of observed stimuli was probably based upon the cognitive networks, self-concept, and mental set of P. No matter how hard we try to be objective, we cannot totally divorce our subjective selves from the process of observing others.

We have previously discussed the theory that each person's mind consists of a network of constructs which consist of linguistic units that can be applied to reality as a means of making sense out of the environment. Keep in mind that these units are unique to the perceiver and are not something found external to P. The self-concept of P also influences the perception of O because P tends to view others as similar or contrasted to him/herself.[2] Some tall persons, for example, may dislike being tall so they assume other tall

23

people also dislike being tall. Self-concept and cognitive constructs both contribute to a mental set of a person which is his/her preparedness to respond in a particular way. If we expect someone to be kind, we watch for some signs of kindness in the behavior of the person. Thus, we are sensitized to behavior which might reflect the antici-

The influence of mental set upon selection of stimuli from a total environment was vividly depicted in a study designed to test the results of police training.[3] Advanced police administration students were asked to view a series of pictures in which scenes of violence were visually matched with neutral scenes. A stereoscope was used in order to present the paired depictions simultaneously. (See figure 2.) Twenty-seven college psychology students reported perceiving an average of 4.03 scenes of violence in contrast to the advanced police administration students who reported an average of 9.37 scenes of violence. Toch and Schulte note that the perception of violence was not a question of selecting and interpreting stimuli but rather an "awareness" in which the subject only "saw" one figure; the second picture never reached the subject because of perceptual mediation. "A momentary exposure of rival fields in a stereoscope presents a perceptual task in which one set of meanings must be elaborated at the expense of another."[4]

FIGURE 2. *One of nine stereograms used in the experiment. (From* Social Perception *edited by H. Toch and H.C. Smith,* © *1968. Reprinted by permission of D. Van Nostrand Company.)*

Once certain stimuli have been selected, P attributes meaning to the observed stimuli and applies linguistic labels. The meaning and linguistic labels are again dependent upon the past and present experiences and future expectations of P. In other words, both the *selection* of perceived stimuli and the *interpretation* of those stimuli are dependent upon the implicit assumptions of P rather than something outside of P which could be referred to as reality. Because person O exists outside of P, his/her existence has no meaning for P except in terms of P's experience. O may have, for example, one hundred individual traits that could be observed, but through the process of selection and generaliza-

tion P derives only twenty traits which may, or may not, reflect O as O perceives his/her self.

Another study of professional training resulting in a mental set demonstrated the negative consequences that can occur in perception of others.[5] This study attempted to determine whether the professional training of clinical psychologists results in their ability to make more accurate social perception than physical scientists. The researcher expected to find that psychologists would be more accurate predictors of college student behavior than physical scientists. Each of the psychologists and physical scientists were provided the age and sex of a college student and, under the condition of maximum information, were provided a transcript of a self-interview. The rather surprising results indicated that the physical scientists were more accurate in their predictions than the psychologists. Both groups received identical stimuli but in the mediation process the psychologists may have attributed special meaning to the material, beyond their capacity to do so with accuracy. Trained to note slight cues of maladjustment, the psychologists may have been led to predict more abnormal behavior than actually performed by the students.

The process of person perception involves the selective observation of certain characteristics of the distal stimulus (O), which are channeled through the sense organs of the proximal stimulus (P), and mediated, or given meaning, in the mind of P. Since the process of perceiving another person is largely dependent upon the characteristics of P, we conclude that the potential of another can be perceived only in light of a subjective assessment of person P.

One of the earliest theorists to attempt an operationalization of trust, Morton Deutsch, emphasized that trust involves more than prediction of another's behavior, it also involves an expectation.[6] The opposite of trust, suspicion, involves an expectation of untrustworthy behavior. Therefore, trust was viewed as an *awareness of another's behavior* as a means of better predicting future behavior *and a mental attitude* that predisposed an individual to expect trust. This expectation, we maintain, is dependent upon personal self-acceptance.

POTENTIAL OF OTHERS

The idea that the potential of another can be realized only in terms of the image of ourselves is enunciated by Carl Rogers in his theory of psychotherapy. Rogers maintains that the successful use of a client-centered approach is closely related to a therapist's personal struggle for growth and integration. "He can be only as 'non-directive' as he has achieved respect for others in his own personality organization."[7] Fundamental to Rogers' client-centered therapy is a belief in each individual's ability to solve his/her own problems and a belief in the personal worth of each individual. These basic assumptions must be implicit in a therapist's way of viewing others.

Each of us develops an expectation of the potential behavior of others in terms of our own potential behaviors modified in terms of perceived personality dimensions of the other. For example, if a friend asks to borrow a book, the situation is assessed in terms of whether or not the lender would see him/herself returning the book, and then the conclusion is modified in terms of the perceived similarity or difference of the potential borrower. If the lender perceives him/herself as being negligent with another's property, he/she will probably be rather cautious about loaning the book. On the other hand, a conscientious person will tend to assess the person in terms of whether the borrower is of similar personality couched in positive overtones. In other words, a person with negative self-acceptance tends to see others in a negative light while the positive person views others in a positive light.

Evidence of this concept was found in early studies by Sheerer[8] and Stock.[9] In both studies, a significant positive relationship was found between expressed attitudes of self-acceptance and expressed attitudes of acceptance of others. This finding was based upon judges' ratings of therapeutic interviews. A third study tested college students, prisoners, and adult YMCA classes on a scale designed to measure self-acceptance and acceptance of others.[10] Once again a positive relationship was found between intrapersonal trust and trust of others.

Another study using a sociometric test to determine *most accepted* and *least accepted* groups in a college dorm, however, failed to report a significant correlation between self-acceptance and acceptance of others for the two groups.[11] In other words, the most accepted students were not necessarily high in self-acceptance and acceptance of others while the least accepted were not necessarily low in these qualities. The study was replicated two years later using scales to measure not only acceptance of self (AS) and acceptance of others (AO) but also a person's estimate of acceptance by others (EA).[12] In order to determine how well each student was actually accepted (AA), each student listed names of five classmates whom he liked best. The findings of the study are rather surprising in light of the previously noted studies. Those students who held a positive AS and AO tended

to EA but were neither more nor less accepted by others (AA). The researcher theorized that these students are not seen by others as needing friendship. Not surprisingly, those students who held a positive AS and a negative AO also tended to EA but were actually rejected by others. In this case the students overestimated acceptability. The students with greatest AA were those who achieved significantly less discrepancy between AS and AO scores than did the least accepted students.

These results add a dimension to our original theory that acceptance of self begets acceptance of others. Namely, a positive evaluation of others tends to be reciprocated. A study conducted to test the relationship between interpersonal trust and teacher effectiveness reflected a reciprocal teacher-student trust upon completion of a semester course.[13] Those instructors who expressed the greatest trust of their students were recipients of the greatest amount of student trust. Conversely, those instructors who expressed "average" or "low" trust of their students received similarly deficient degrees of student trust.[14] Thus, as we accept others, others accept us, reinforcing our original positive self-acceptance. On the other hand, negative acceptance of others results in rejection, reinforcing the negatively held self-perception.

Further verification of this theory is offered by Wiest who measured the self-esteem of elementary and junior high school youth.[15] The results suggested that the higher a person's self-esteem, the more positive the correlation between his/her feelings toward others and his/her perceptions of their feelings toward him/her. The researcher concluded the generalization that persons like those who they think like them and dislike those who they think dislike them, is most strongly manifested in persons with high self-esteem.

SELF-ESTEEM VIS-À-VIS SELF-ACCEPTANCE

We have pointed out that high intrapersonal trust is beneficial to an individual and to his/her perception of others. In the previous chapter we defined intrapersonal trust as self-acceptance measured by the similarity between ideal self traits and actual self traits. Closely related is the concept of self-esteem which is the value judgment attached to self-perception. Conceptual confusion between self-esteem and self-acceptance may be partially accounted for by the fact that a person identified as high in self-acceptance will generally have positive self-esteem. We maintain, however, that persons who are truly in touch with themselves will be able to recognize strengths and weaknesses, virtues and faults in their psycho-physical make-up. A person with an extremely high self-esteem may have defensively hidden his/her weaknesses and faults.

A study of the relationship of self-perception to adjustment or defensiveness revealed that persons whose self-descriptions closely agreed with expert judges' descriptions rated more highly in adjustment and were less defensive on a perceptual-defense test than persons who agreed less closely with judges.[16] Somewhat naively, the person with extremely high self-esteem assumes a personal competence but fails to see the same potential in others. At the opposite extreme, the person with low self-esteem fails to recognize his/her own strengths and overestimates the potential of others. The first person trusts no one but him/herself to achieve important tasks, the second person prefers to trust everyone but him/herself in accomplishment of tasks. Persons with a desirable level of intrapersonal trust should not be on either end of the self-esteem continuum. Because of a willingness to accept themselves with all their inherent positive and negative qualities, they are also psychologically set to accept similar combinations of valued traits in others.

RECIPROCAL TRUST

The correlative chain we have established thus far is that intrapersonal trust provides the psychological foundation for perceiving potential in others. The effect of expressing faith in others is that others reciprocate these feelings through feedback. In the classic study of leadership styles, White and Lippitt found that when boys were treated autocratically, they rebelled against the rules, fought among themselves, and generally misbehaved.[17] When they were lead democratically, however, they were compatible, reasonably well behaved, and productive in accomplishment of tasks. A series of studies reviewed by Carl Rogers in his book *On Becoming a Person* lends further support to the view that an attitude of trust can foster a growth-promoting relationship.[18] One study of particular interest found that children of parents with warm, equalitarian attitudes demonstrated accelerated intellectual development, more originality, more emotional security, and less excitability than children from other types of homes.[19] The effects of interpersonal trust will be further amplified in the following chapters. The idea we want to convey at this point is that we can project these attitudes of democratic acceptance to the degree that we can be sensitively aware of and acceptant toward our own feelings. In the words of Rogers, "The degree to which I can create relationships which facilitate the growth of others as separate persons is a measure of the growth I have achieved in myself."[20]

LOW SELF-ACCEPTANCE—REJECTION OF OTHER'S POTENTIAL

Thus far we have focused primarily upon the desirability of positive self-acceptance as a means of seeing potential in others. We have also noted that as people perceive positive potential in others the positive expectations are reciprocated. Conversely, those with low self-acceptance tend to perceive others either as untrustworthy or as trustworthy in their own behavior but unreliable as a source of reciprocal trust.

The first case was illustrated earlier in the chapter with the example of a person asking to borrow a book. An unreliable person (P) tends to project his/her own behavior onto the other person (O). Therefore, if P has forgotten to return other people's books in the past, he/she anticipates O also to be negligent. As a result, P is unwilling to trust O with the book. Projection of one's own weaknesses and faults seems to be a technique used more by persons with high self-esteem than those with low self-esteem, however. In theory, if a person has low self-esteem, he/she expects negative behavioral effects and negative feedback from others. Respected others may be perceived as being capable of much better potential. In other words, the low self-esteem person says, "No one could be as bad as I," and therefore does not project inadequacies on others. In contrast, the high self-esteem person may feel very uncomfortable upon learning of his/her own weakness and may have a strong need to project the weakness onto respected others or to others in his/her reference group. The high self-esteem person says, "If this has happened to me it surely has happened to others just as good or better than I."

Support for this position was found in a study conducted by Bramel.[21] Eighty-four males were divided into two groups, one with high self-esteem and the other group with low. Each subject was then given false information about himself of a theoretically undesirable nature in the form of emotional arousal scores. The main difference between the two groups was that this negative information would be less expected by those subjects having high self-esteem. Each of the subjects was paired with another subject at the time this negative information was given to him. He was then asked to predict the score of the subject with whom he was paired. As had been hypothesized, those with positive self-esteem predicted undesirable scores for the other pair member. Those with negative self-esteem tended to predict somewhat more desirable scores for their partners. The results of this study suggest that when we receive negative feedback from reliable others we may either assign the same trait information to others or internalize the feedback with the determination based, at least to some degree, upon self-concept.

A number of other studies have been conducted to examine response to negative feedback.[22] There appears to be strong evidence that persons with average or above average degrees of self-esteem can accept criticism as a means of improving behavior. If an instructor in a speech class, for example, offers a critique of a student performance, most students will use the feedback to improve their speaking ability and consequently their self-concept as communicators.[23] Unfortunately, those most in need of improvement often use the information as reinforcement of the belief that they are not competent as communicators. Furthermore, evaluation from others tends to have a spreading effect.[24] If a speaker is told that he/she used poor gestures, he/she may mentally spread the evaluation to related areas such as the entire act of speaking in front of groups. Conversely, positive reinforcement of certain behaviors may also spread. Homans cites the example that a child perceived by a teacher as doing well in math and spelling will also be perceived to do well in reading.[25] The effect may be the child's actual belief in his/her reading ability and consequent behavior of doing well.

Based upon this information, an instructor might be well advised to provide as much positive reinforcement as possible for student behaviors.[26] A significant limitation to the principle, however, is that the positive evaluation may not be believed. We previously noted that persons with low self-esteem accept negative feedback because it is congruent with previously held self beliefs. Students at the University of Minnesota were asked to identify the three most confident and three least confident students in their speech class.[27] Each set of six students was then interviewed by the researcher and told that they were

You are really a nice guy, Fred, but . . .

selected on the basis of high confidence and poise. A written post-test of speaker confidence was administered during the following week. The results indicated that those initially low in confidence did not improve in confidence any more than those initially found to be high or average in levels of confidence.

These studies combine to depict rather dismal prospects for the person low in self-regard. Negative information is believed and used to reinforce the negative self-concept, positive information is not believed since it is incongruent with previous convictions. This principle will be elaborated on in the following chapter. The central issue to keep in mind at this point is that low self-concept will inevitably result in an inability to perceive others as a source of benefit to one's self.

The only way out of this dilemma is for O to accept P as a human being with potential for resolving his/her problems, to avoid negative *or* positive evaluative statements, and when feedback is requested to offer it with genuine honesty. Or turning the issue around, if P wishes to achieve improved self-acceptance he/she must begin with an acceptance of others.

I AND THOU

As others perceive acceptance, they feed back acceptance which fosters a sense of well being and self-esteem. The ultimate person-to-person communicative relationship is described by Martin Buber as an I and Thou experience.[28] Each person experiences the other in the fullness of his/her being. Facades and roles are stripped away as each person faces the other real in his/her existence. Buber carries the idea one step further than we have defined it so far in our discussion of self-concept and intrapersonal trust. The meaning of a person's existence is found in the community of person to person. An individual cannot become a whole self except through dialogue with another.

This dialogue takes on mystical qualities as two separate individuals merge in a mutual sharing of existence. For Buber, the ultimate meaning in life, the experiencing of God, is found in the merging existence of I and Thou. Needless to say, the type of relationship advocated by Buber is not the common discussion with your neighbor or loved one about daily happenings. Most communication occurs in the world of I – It relations. We talk about It in the context of time, space, and causality. It is explained by Paul Pfuetze as an attitude of common sense and science.[29] The scientist seizes an object of percep-

tion, studies it, compares and classifies it, establishes it in a proper order, and establishes a general statement regarding its relation in time and space. "This is the world of security, of predictable events, of fixed laws and understood connections which enable men/women to form a reasonable plan by which to build, sustain, and equip organized social living."[30] Such knowledge allows us to "progress" by conquering and controlling nature. But the development of these powers decreases an individual's potential to be a fully functioning being. The language of man/woman is dominated by reference to he, she, they, and it while I and Thou diminish in relevance for existence.

As long as an individual lives in the I–It, he/she lacks the fullness of reality. We are human only to the extent that we live in dialogue with others. Recall that trust has been defined as the reliance upon another in order to achieve an uncertain objective in a risky situation. An I – It relationship seeks to remove the uncertainty and risk by objectively viewing reality by a separation in time and space. We are safest when we engage in dialogue about things that occurred there and then, when we view each other as objects of manipulation, analyzation, and control; and when we allow the rationality of our considered acts to dominate the irrationality of our totality of existence.

RISK IN RELATIONSHIPS

An I – Thou relationship, in contrast, requires the acceptance of uncertainty and risk. The whole of one's being is involved. I meet You directly in our present existence. Time and space fade as we are totally immersed in mutual relations, whether spoken or silent. The relationship is characterized by love and a genuineness of response and responsibility. We risk everything in the quest of God, the meaning of life, a positive relationship with another, or perhaps something even less understood. We risk the concreteness of self for the abstractness of metaphysics.

In considering whether to risk ourselves in dialogue with another, we weigh the risk in terms of the assumptions we hold about our fellow man/woman. Buber's philosophy was strongly influenced by the religious teachings of Chassidism which maintained that redemption lay in loving deeds, humility and simplicity, and most importantly a devotion to God and man/woman in the common life. In other words, the foundation of Buber's philosophy is a belief in the positive value of a person in dialogue with another person irrespective of external roles or status. Person with person can be nothing but good because between You and I exists the spirit of God.

For many of us the religious fervor of Buber is not as important as the assumption that I can be human only to the extent that you can be. Psychologically and philosophically we are bound together in the immediacy of our existence. If I want to exist as a fully functioning person, I must risk myself in relationship with You. In order to find the courage to assume the risk, or from another perspective, in order to reduce the risk to manageable proportions, I must perceive a positive potential in You and be acceptant of myself as an I worthy of being in relation with You. To repeat the recurrent theme of this chapter, I perceive your potential in terms of my own self-acceptance. Part of the desirability of perceiving potential in you is the benefit I receive when I see that you accept me. To paraphrase Buber, I can say I only to the extent that I can say You.

Willingness to rely upon You can be regarded as interpersonal trust, which is the focus of the next chapter.

SUMMARY

We have emphasized throughout this chapter that we inevitably perceive others through our personal, subjective filters. Limited bits of information are selected from the environment based upon cognitive networks and self-concept which combine to provide a mental set for reception. Once the bits of stimuli have been relayed to the brain from the sensors, meaning and linguistic labels are applied in order to make "sense" out of the data. Therefore, the perception of others as worthy of trust involves a sensory awareness of their behavior and a mental attitude of expecting trust. Others can only be as trusting as one allows them to be through his/her expectations and selective observations.

The expectation of others' potential behavior is couched in terms of our own behavior and modified in terms of the perceived personality of the others. Therefore, persons with negative self-acceptance permit others to be viewed in a positive light. Positive acceptance is then generally reciprocated by the others.

We maintain that self-esteem may reflect defensively hidden weakness and an assumption of personal competence not attributed to others. Low self-esteem results in a failure to recognize personal worth and overestimation of others' potential. Persons with a desirable level of trust should not fall on either extreme end of the self-esteem continuum.

A person with low self-acceptance tends to believe negative feedback but fails to use it for improvement of behavior. Furthermore, feedback referring to a specific behavior is spread to related behavioral areas. Positive feedback to the person with low self-acceptance is not believed and again fails to result in behavioral improvement. The only alternative for the person appears to be striving for increased acceptance of others through a gradual risking of self in a personal encounter with others. Through nonevaluative feedback a better realization of self in relation to others can be achieved.

Interpersonal Trust as a Benefit to Self

In chapters 2 and 3 we discussed *intra-personal* trust as a benefit to self and as a benefit to seeing potential in others. We have maintained that each person is free to choose his/her acts which constitute his/her being or existence. The choice of acts is based upon past experiences and an anticipation of the future. With this choice goes a responsibility in which each person must accept the consequences of his/her acts. Given this responsibility for self-development you may justifiably ask, why should I risk my psychic well-being by trusting others? This chapter seeks to answer that question in terms of the benefits to self a person gains from *interpersonal* trust.

In the beginning of chapter 2 we mentioned that a sense of self is partially gained from an inner dialogue with self and a dialogue with others. Central to the development of self is an inner realization of self embedded in a perceived environment. In turn, each of us has a need to check out our perceptions of self and reality by means of communication with others. The need for validation of our existence through interaction with others has been referred to as an interpersonal imperative.[1]

INTERPERSONAL IMPERATIVE

This imperative to be recognized varies in intensity and mode of expression from person to person. All of us have known people who have a difficult time maintaining eye contact with one person because they are regularly looking around for other people to say "hi" to. These people seem to have a strong need for recognition by many other people. Others seem to be satisfied with relatively few friends to interact with and to be recognized by. One theorist has suggested that each person has a need for moving toward others which ranges from mild attraction to love.[2] A person needing affection and approval may be contrasted to the recluse who moves away from others. The hermit might appear to be an exception to the interpersonal imperative, except case histories of people who have withdrawn from society invariably note that they make friends and interact with animals, birds, and assorted pets. There seems to be a need for a response even if the respondent is not human. The *amount* of affection needed by an individual may vary inversely with the amount received as a child. When given large amounts of attention and affection in the formative years of childhood, a person may have a lower need for affection as an adult while another person who receives small doses of affection in the early years may have a high need for affection as an adult.

By affection we are referring to feedback, validation, responses, or simply a focus of attention. In other words, our previous example of the person who is constantly looking around for someone else to interact with may have a high need for affection. No matter which end of the need continuum we consider, however, everyone needs regularized validation of existence from others.

The *type* of affection received during the child's formative years may also have an influence on the type of affection sought during adolescence or adulthood. For example, if the parent regularly provides affection as a means of rewarding certain behaviors of the child and withholds affection at other times, the affection may be regarded as *conditional.* Providing praise for high grades, hugging the baby after she smiles, cheering a home run are all positive forms of conditional affection. Less desirable forms include telling the child that "Daddy won't love you if you wet the bed," or "If you strike out, I'll never come to watch you play." *Unconditional* affection includes the traditional good night kiss, a hug in the middle of the day for no particular reason, and an over-all warm acceptance. It is safe to suggest that all children receive some degree of both conditional and unconditional affection from others. The significant consideration is the ratio of conditional to unconditional affection. If you received 80 percent conditional and 20 percent unconditional affection from others during your formative years, then you may strive for unconditional affection as an adolescent or adult. Curiously enough, however, your behavior may primarily draw conditional affection. Thus, as a result of childhood experiences, a person may develop a need for one type of affection but actually elicit the other type due to a learned mode of behavior.

This is based upon the premise that we all like to receive affection from others. As children, we learn how to gain affection from others while developing somewhat of a blind spot for how to achieve the less commonly received type of affection. As adults, we follow the well-learned path of behavior while actually needing the path not traveled. A "workaholic" may be an example of a person who gives up unconditional affection from friends, family, and associates because of an overdependence upon conditional affection received as a result of success on the job. The person spends every moment thinking about his/her job as a means of gaining sought for affection. Meanwhile, he/she may actually fail to achieve the needed unconditional affection or may be unable to recognize sources of sought for affection and validation.

In some cases, gaining validation from *significant* other people may be difficult to achieve. The significance of an other is based upon the perceived importance of the other for the individual. Role or status of others may or may not be relevant in the determination of the significance of others since significance is determined by the importance another has for the developmental existence of a particular individual. Significant others for many of us include parents, siblings, close friends, sex partners, groups to which we aspire, and perhaps rivals and enemies to whom we reactively respond. In Ralph Ellison's fascinating novel, *The Invisible Man,* the black protagonist seeks validation from whites but is constantly denied an existence by responses to his role and race rather than to him as a person.[3] Eventually Ellison's tragic figure concludes that since no one can see him as an existent being, he is invisible.

At times the need for validation can be expressed and found in nonverbal behavior. Waving or nodding at a neighbor is a socially approved mode of seeking a response. Physically attacking a significant other is certainly a less acceptable mode of requesting validation. At an upper-class high school where lower-class students were being bused, apparently senseless acts of violence occurred. Students representing the upper-class majority were attacked in isolated corridors by lower-class minority students with whom they had never before interacted. The resultant scuffle inevitably resulted in physical harm to both parties and some form of punishment by school officials. The motive for these acts of aggression seemed to be missing. However, one way of analyzing the incidents is in terms of the interpersonal imperative. The upper-class students were, in general, secure financially, psychologically, and scholastically. They were not threatened by the presence of the lower-class students because of a secure existence. Therefore, unlike schools where middle-class and lower-class students were integrated, few defensive interactions occured. The lower-class students could stand on their heads in the hallways and their presence would still be largely ignored. In the classrooms their contributions, for good or ill, were not a threat to the secure students' academic achievement so once again they were largely ignored. For at least a small portion of these students, all attempts to achieve validation were denied by others. As a final effort to gain a response, representatives of the secure group were physically attacked. In fighting back they validated the existence of the tragically estranged individuals. Even the school officials finally gave the minority students sought for recognition by punishment. Physical harm and expulsion may seem like high prices to pay for validation, but this example is illustrative of the strong impetus the need for validation can produce.

Over a hundred years ago Dostoyevsky wrote a fascinating portrayal of a wretched individual in *Notes from Underground.*[4] Time and again the man fails in his attempts to gain a response from significant others. Upon passing a bar he observes a person being thrown through the window. He perceives a chance to exist: "I envied that ejected gentleman so much that I entered the tavern . . . thinking: 'Maybe I could pick a fight too and be thrown out the window.' "[5] Eventually, he leaves, having failed in his attempt to pick a fight. The man from whom he sought a response had quickly thwarted his quest for validation. "He grabbed me by the shoulders and, without a word, picked me up, and setting me down a bit further away, passed by as if I didn't exist."[6]

A third example of the extreme ends to which some people may go in order to gain a response is found in Harry Chapin's depiction of a shooting incident that occurred at the University of Texas.[7] A young university student by the name of Charles Whitman climbed to the observation deck located on the twenty-ninth floor of the administration building and proceeded to fire down randomly on the people below. Before the tragic incident was concluded, thirteen people lay dead or dying and thirty-one were injured in one of the most savage one-man shooting sprees in the history of American crime.[8] In the "Sniper" the motive of this bizarre incident is attributed to the lack of validation. Whitman asks, in the powerful verse of Harry Chapin, "Am I? I am a lover who's never been kissed. Am I? I am a fighter who's not made a fist. Am I? If I'm alive then there's so much I've missed. How do I know I exist? Are you listening to me? Are you listening to me? Am I?" The answer is ultimately provided in his death, "Am I? Though you have put your fire inside me. You've given me an answer can't you see. I was. I am. And now, *I will be.*"[9]

Fortunately, most people do not need to go to such tragic ends to gain a sense of self. However, when the selection of a skimpy bikini or a worn, faded pair of blue jeans is viewed in terms of a request for validation, we recognize that all of us behave in unique and sometimes strange ways as a means of gaining response from valued others.

Responses as a means of validation are what we have previously referred to as feedback. Advocates of transactional analysis add stroking as yet another synonym for validating another person's existence.[10] Among the several types of strokes which can be identified, "warm fuzzies" are those positive strokes which come in the form of compliments, smiles, hugs, kisses, friendly pats, or perhaps simply a kind word of recognition. Generally speaking, all people like to receive warm fuzzies from others and are often rather embarrassed or reluctant to give them to others. We suggest that when a person's communication with others is uncertain or confused, when one fails to find the right words for another person, when a relationship seems to falter, the best alternative may be a warm fuzzy in the form of a simple touch or embrace. Prescriptively speaking, when in doubt, stroke. However, some strokes are not so pleasant to receive. "Cold pricklies" are the negative responses we give in the form of snide remarks, hits, bites, kicks or "put downs." They are generally used to punish the behavior of the other person but still serve the function of validating the other person's exist-

ence. Except in extreme form, any type of stroke is better than no strokes at all. The commonly used phrase by practitioners of transactional analysis is that if a person doesn't get strokes "the spine shrivels up and the person dies."

COMMUNICATION SUPPRESSION

Giffin and Heider have posited that regularized patterns of communication suppression in the formative period of two to six years of age may result in communication anxiety.[11] Communication suppression refers to the failure to respond to the child's communication attempts. For example, the child's request for a drink of water is answered by instructions to go watch television. When the child attempts to show a scribbled drawing to the father, the only response is a grunt as he continues to read the evening paper. The child wanders off to show the picture to the mother who is attempting to prepare dinner. Once again an attempt to gain recognition is crushed by the preoccupied behavior of the parent. All of us can recognize the inevitability of occasionally ignoring a child's communication attempts. A person would get nothing else accomplished if every scrambled question of a three-year-old was answered to the child's satisfaction. Suppression of communication as used here occurs on a regularized basis when a request for recognition is neither confirmed nor denied, but is simply ignored. In searching for a self, the child's attempts to gain validation are ignored. Since the child is tied to the parent in these early years, he/she trusts the parent's communication as a significant other. Gradually the child becomes estranged from self and places a low value on his/her personal worth.

As the child advances in age, new significant others may attempt to alter the previously adopted self-image. However, by then the child is mentally set to expect negative evaluations from others. We maintained in the previous chapter that a person with low self-acceptance avoids interaction with others for fear of receiving negatively perceived feedback. Positive feedback from others, on the other hand, is not believed because of the previously established mental set toward self and others. In general, the person with low self-acceptance is in a bind. Negative feedback is believed but disliked and avoided; positive feedback is not believed or is perceptually distorted.

An initial answer to the question of why we ought to trust others is that the potential response of others can help reaffirm, clarify, or perhaps alter a previously held perception of self in reference to others. Whether we agree with the preceived communication from others or not, by exposing ourselves to others we have the opportunity to gain additional insight into our communicative effects upon others.

SYMBOLIC INTERACTIONISM

A second part to the issue of trusting others as a benefit to self can be found in the writings of George Herbert Mead and his followers. Mead maintained that we are a product of significant others.[12] As we interact with others we gain a sense of self from the responses of others. Since the response others provide is a reflection of themselves, we are constantly seeing ourselves through the perceptually distorted reflections of others. These reflections from each of our significant others combine to form a *generalized other* which becomes the self. In other words, we are a composite of all those who form our significant others, e.g., our mother, father, brother, sister, best friend, peer group, and occupational associates.

For Mead, self is constituted by a dialogue between "I" and "Me." The "I" phase of self derives from first-hand, unorganized aspects of experiencing. "I went to the grocery store and talked with Sally" is an example of experiencing self as subject of experiences. The "Me" phase of self is gained by assuming the role of others and responding from their perspective as an object to self. In the playful years of childhood, dual roles are assumed—that of our own and that of some other person. While playing alone the child mimics the parent by saying, "Billy, you're a bad boy. If you don't stop playing in your food, I'll spank you." "OK, mother, I'll be good." The child is both mother and child as a means of exploring the attitudes held by others toward himself. Eventually the child transcends individual roles to the role of the generalized other. The norms, attitudes, and values of others are internalized and in turn determine the child's choice of acts and perception of reality. We noted in the previous chapter that a child's being is determined by his/her choice of acts which in turn are determined in large part by taking on the roles of significant others during the formative years. Each of the separate roles is eventually blended into an individualized collage of being or existence. The parental admonition to select one's friends carefully is well founded since the child figuratively becomes a reflection of his/her peers. What the admonition ignores is the saliency of each significant other. Since the parent interacts more frequently and is physically tied closer to the child than any of the peers, the parent's behavior will in most cases carry heavier weight of influence than that of the peers. The old saying, "Like father, like son," is to a great degree true.

Since a person's self is largely determined by significant others, it follows that a consciousness of one's self is achieved in proportion to the frequency with which one participates in interactions with others. Thus, for Mead, man/woman's basic nature is not revealed by intrapersonal communication but from his/her characteristic reactions to and with others. A person needs others in order to be him/herself.

The ideas of Mead's school of symbolic interactionism rest on three premises, according to Herbert Blumer: first, that humans act toward things on the basis of the *meaning* the things have for them; second, that the *meaning* of such things is *derived from interaction* with others; and third, that these *meanings are modified by the interpretive process* used in dealing with the experiences with the things encountered.[13] In terms of self, the meaning of existence is gained from interpersonal communication and modified by one's own perceptual process of dealing with experiences.

The uniqueness of a person is that he/she is not a slave to past experiences, nor is he/she entirely dependent upon the views of others. We reflect upon the past as a means of perceiving and interpreting our present condition, anticipate the future by taking on the roles of others, and mindfully choose our acts accordingly. The concept sometimes applied to our symbolizing capacity is *time binding*. We can instantaneously recall the past and anticipate the future as a determination for the present by means of symbolic thought. Overt behaviors can be delayed while we predict the possible consequences of our proposed acts in terms of others' possible responses; thus, time is bridged by thought.

Why trust others? Two possible reasons have been offered so far. Others provide an external perception of the individual as a means of clarification, amplification, and alteration of self. Second, interaction with others provides insight into how others respond to conditions and events. This increased insight allows the individual to better assume the role of the other in consideration of selected acts. The better an individual can accurately assume the role of others, the better he/she can select appropriate acts as a determination of self.

VALIDATION OF REALITY

A third benefit to self gained by trusting others is an opportunity to check out our perception of reality. How does a child know that a light is dim unless enough trusted others consistently tell him/her that it is dim? How can a teenager know that a new rock song is "good" unless others confirm the value judgment? How can a plant supervisor know that a decision to lay off workers is the best solution to a problem of costs unless he/she checks out his/her perception with others? We suggest that all reality is grounded in a continuum of probability. Only by checking with trusted others can we achieve some degree of certainty, probability, possibility, or plausability about reality as a basis for determination of our acts.

FEEDBACK RELIABILITY

Strangely enough, a fourth justification of trusting others as a benefit to self is that feedback cannot be relied upon unless the other person is trusted. In other words, information about reality can be trusted to the extent that the person providing the information is trusted. This principle works in a reciprocal fashion. Assume Kathy distrusts Sue and has three pieces of information which could be useful to Sue. Because Kathy distrusts Sue only two bits of Kathy's information are revealed. At the same time, Sue perceives Kathy holding back information so Sue shares only one of her pieces of information. Kathy thinks to herself, "I knew Sue couldn't be trusted, I'm glad I didn't reveal all my information." A similar thought reinforces Sue's previously held conviction. Thus, both girls are deprived of potentially helpful information. A study of trust among co-workers found that members of a research institute who trusted each other understood the others' positions more accurately if they communicated about relevant issues.[14] However, if they did not trust the person with whom they talked, communication did not increase accuracy. In terms of our example, Sue is motivated to communicate with Kathy and if Sue distrusts Kathy, she will communicate in such a way as to conceal information from Kathy about her own attitudes.[15]

When viewed from strictly an information exchange perspective, then, trust of others is important in order to have some confidence in the data and in order to gain the maximum amount of available data. A problem in many organizations is lateral communication in the hierarchy. News is generally passed up the hierarchy as a means of enhancing the subordinate's position in the eyes of the superior.[16] In turn, superiors generally pass news down to subordinates in order to achieve organizational objectives. Neither the superior nor the subordinate is threatened by the other since their status levels differ. When information must be exchanged between individuals on the same hierarchical level, however, the condition changes. Each person is motivated to exchange information as a means of solving mutual

tasks but also feels the need to withhold vital bits of information in order to be the first to achieve the solution and to reap the rewards of increased status. Perhaps as a student you have been faced with this mixed motivation in some of your classes. In preparing for a final exam, do you study with other class members as a means of benefiting from mutual exchange of knowledge or do you withhold some of your special insights in order to achieve top ranking in the class?

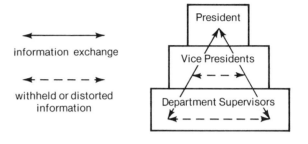

FIGURE 3

Many teachers try to encourage student cooperation by removing or reducing the competition for class ranking and grades. In a similar manner organizations often stress the importance of interdepartmental cooperation while downplaying the stress of competition. This is difficult to achieve, however, if there are four department supervisors and only one vice-presidential position to be filled. A partial answer to the problem might be a reward system for cooperation, but the limitation of this principle can be easily recognized by means of analogy. Assume you are a coach of a basketball team and two players are competing for starting center. One has great defensive skills and the other has a deft shooting ability. Furthermore, assume that you observe one of these players helping the other with his specialty. Eventually one player, through the aid of the other, becomes competent in both offense and defense. As coach do you reward the cooperative player or the most competent one with the starting position? The answer is obvious, you go with the winner. You know that from the outset and so do the players. In a similar manner, the organization is going to reward the person who can successfully accomplish the job.

Prisoner's Dilemma

The combination of cooperative and competitive needs can be regarded as a mixed motive and has been operationalized in a mathematical game theory regarded by some as a prisoner's dilemma. The game rules are established by explaining to participants that two criminals have been called in for questioning and placed in separate rooms.

Each prisoner is told that he will receive a reduced sentence if he confesses. If he doesn't confess and the other prisoner does, however, a stiff sentence will be handed down. If both confess they will receive light sentences and if neither confesses they will be charged with some fabricated crime. Figure 4 represents the outcome of each prisoner's decision of whether or not to confess.

Prisoner B

		Not Confess	Confess
Prisoner A	Not Confess	1 yr, 1 yr	5 yr, 6 mo
	Confess	6 mo, 5 yr	2 yr, 2 yr

FIGURE 4

The first number in each cell of the figure represents the reward or penalty to prisoner A, the second number the outcome to B. For example, if both confess they are imprisoned for two years each, if A confesses but B refuses A will be sentenced to six months and B to five years of imprisonment, and so on. As you can see the outcome is weighted heavily in favor of confessing and the punishment for not confessing is dependent upon the behavior of the other person. This procedure is regarded as a non-zero-sum game since the outcome of one person's decision is not entirely counter to the outcome for the other person.

If you were to match pennies with a friend and every time they were identical you won and every time they differed, your friend won, the game would be called zero-sum since the reward of one person would always match the penalty of the other person. Zero-sum games represent, then, diametrically opposed conflicts of interest (see fig. 5).

You

		Heads	Tails
Friend	Heads	+1¢, −1¢	−1¢, +1¢
	Tails	−1¢, +1¢	+1¢, −1¢

FIGURE 5. *Zero sum game*

In all our examples of mixed motivation, however, the "players" did not have an easy decision of whether or not to trust others absolutely with a clear-cut win-lose outcome. We maintain that in most personal relationships certain advantages can be won or lost by making either choice since

the interests of all parties partially diverge and partially coincide.[17]

In the prisoner's dilemma game the outcome was heavily influenced by the game maker (interogator). Many situations involving mixed motivation provide a small gain if each player cooperates, a significant gain if one person competes and the other cooperates, and a sizable loss if both players compete. Figure 6 is representative of the dilemma described in our earlier example of four department executives exchanging information. If all of them cooperate and trust one another their gain will be small but equal. If one of them decides to hold vital information while collecting the others' cooperative exchange, the immediate reward will be much larger but gained at

O

		B_1	B_2
P	A_1	5, 5	−10, 10
	A_2	10, −10	−5, −5

FIGURE 6

the expense of the others. Let us assume that all of them decide they are unable to trust each other. Then they all end up losing a little. The dilemma they face in this situation of known competitiveness is that they "can't" trust the other for fear of losing even more. In the language of game theory they have reached a "saddle point" in which any change in position by an individual results in a deterioration condition. Without forced compliance, i.e., company edict or an opportunity to communicate, they are probably doomed to failure.

At the same time, the cooperative scheme may not truly reflect trust of one another. The choice of A_1 (or B_1) may be the only rational behavior since A_2 (or B_2) will inevitably result in retaliation from the others. If one of the department executives "rips off" the others, what do you think will be the behavior of the others on subsequent choices of behavior? A decision to be competitive may solve an immediate objective, but what happens to the competitor when he/she must face the victims of the future? A decision to choose A_1 (or B_1) may be simply a matter of inevitable coalition for survival.

Figure 6 is a typical pay-off matrix used in research on strategies. Usually the pay off is in terms of monetary rewards, and players are tempted to deviate from the cooperative alliance by increasing the values in the competitive cells A_2 (or B_2). Direct communication between players is often prohibited or severely restricted in order to require each player to evaluate the other's intent by observation of choices. The basis of a player's behavior is said to be a product of P's generalized expectation of trustworthiness of the other and previous experience with the specific situation.[18] Assuming no previous experience, P has only a generalized attitude toward the trustworthiness of others as a criterion for the choice. Given experience from previous trials, P trusts O if O behaves in a way that would allow P to take advantage of him/her.

Cooperative behavior is more quickly achieved when players are given an opportunity to communicate than if not given an opportunity,[19] if they are provided the results of sequential, as opposed to simultaneous play,[20] and if the instructions emphasize that the players are partners in contrast to competitors.[21] One interesting variation of the game did not permit the players to know the effect of each response.[22] Players were informed of the results for themselves after having made a choice but not the effect upon the other player's score. Over a series of trials, twenty-six of thirty-four pairs achieved a stable sequence of giving each player nothing but gains $(A_1 B_1)$. In answer to how they figured out the best combination of behaviors, twenty-nine of the players reported using the response of their partner's behavior. Trial-to-trial stability was believed to indicate a response which yielded gains and trial-to-trial variability meant losses. Significantly, this assumption about behavior works as long as one player is willing to set aside his/her concern for gains and losses temporarily and to adopt an information-seeking role. In terms of interpersonal communication, P and O can only achieve a mutually beneficial relationship if P is willing to sacrifice momentary loss in favor of long-term gain. The rationale of P must be that in risking self by trusting O, the communicated trust will be reciprocated by O.

We have attempted to provide you with a brief introduction to a vast amount of experimental research on game theory. Several scholars have been critical of the application of the prisoner's dilemma games to trust. Earlier we suggested that cooperative behavior may be more representative of a coalition or compliance than trust. Even Deutsch, who originally formulated the relationship of cooperation to trust, has noted that cooperative play may be representative of despair, conformity, impulsiveness, or some social norm.[23] One could also question how many social situations resemble the dichotomous options and distributions of outcomes found in the prisoner's dilemma pattern.[24] Finally we must question the generalizability of laboratory research to the "real" world.

In spite of the aforementioned limitations, some generalizations based upon game theory

research merit review. Additional self benefits to interpersonal trust include: failure to trust others may result in a competitive saddle point in which everyone loses and runs the risk of even more significant loss if their position is altered; willingness to accept initial loss due to trusting others may eventually pay dividends from others' dependence upon your reliability; and an expectation of others' trustworthiness begets trusting behavior.

Finally, in answering the question, "Why trust others?" we will explore the therapeutic effects. As we trust others and they in turn trust us, the resultant relationship can have a positive beneficial effect on us.

REDUCING EFFECTS OF TRAUMATIC EXPERIENCES

If you stop and think for a minute you probably can recall an acquaintance who apparently suffered rather severe circumstances at some earlier stage in life. His/her way of looking at the world or of responding to others indicates that he/she has been hurt—suffered some traumatic experience. As a result, he/she has grown suspicious of certain kinds of people or circumstances. He/she uses defensive mechanisms; avoids people or attacks them verbally before knowing how they perceive him/her. We can say that because of these earlier traumatic experiences he/she has become very sensitive (sensitized) to the possibility of this hurt being repeated.

We do not mean to deny that experience is a good teacher and that you should not avoid sitting on a hot stove after you've been properly burned. This point is: all stoves are not hot. All circumstances that remind you of a time when you were hurt are not the same. Our concern is with the person who overgeneralizes the trauma —who is afraid of all or most people, who trusts almost nobody, and who tends to avoid interaction even when it could be of great benefit to him/her.

Careful investigations of learning behavior have demonstrated that people can reduce such inordinate fears by approaching feared situations carefully and learning to discriminate more clearly those that will hurt them from those that won't.[25] In this way their *unreasonable* expectations of hurt can be diminshed.

In such a manner you should re-evaluate your lack of trust of other people. Do not throw all caution to the winds, but carefully observe people to note who can be properly trusted. An excellent approach is to note who is willing to trust you.

When others trust us—are willing to rely on us in a situation where they could lose something of value to them—we should take a very careful look at them and consider returning the favor. As we see that we can trust them with little inconsequential things, we will find ourselves losing some of our fear that they might hurt us. In this way the effects of earlier traumatic experiences can be reduced and we can interact with others in ways that give us increased satisfaction.

ESTABLISHING MORE SATISFYING RELATIONSHIPS

As we find that others trust us, we tend to gain a more satisfying view of ourselves. Our self-image is improved and our world looks brighter.[26] In addition, we tend to gain a clearer sense of what is real and what isn't. When we are in a condition of constant fear or suspicion of others as a result of some severely traumatic experience, we ordinarily sense that our view of the world is unrealistic, but at the time we cannot afford to test this dimly perceived reality. We see other people trusting people, and we wish we could, but because of excessive fear we can hardly afford to trust anybody! By noting who trusts us and offering little bits of our trust in return, we can move to a position where our sense of reality is more concrete. Thus, we risk a little to test the results and very carefully observe what really happens—*not being sorely limited by what we fear might happen.*

Experiences of persons who work with groups in trying to improve human relations have demonstrated that a climate of trust by members of a group can have a beneficial effect on persons who are very much afraid to interact with others. Sometimes such a group atmosphere has been called a "supportive climate."[27] Carl Rogers has suggested that this atmosphere provides "psychological safety" for a needlessly fearful person to re-evaluate his/her need for defenses and to experiment with less strained or tense interpersonal behavior.[28]

When we find that other people really trust us, life's panorama of pleasure, fun, and shared excitement opens up before us. Some of the most enjoyable times in life occur when two people together risk something important to both of them, relying on each other to carry it off. Here we have in mind such shared experiences as playing together as a tennis team; or helping each other learn to ski; or in a much more serious but still very exciting vein, sharing a marriage or raising a family. Mutual trust can open the way to a very important part of life's potential.

It probably does not need to be stated that without letting oneself interact very much with another person it is impossible to establish a very satisfying interpersonal relationship. As you find others showing trust in you the opportunity to relate to them in important ways will be apparent. As they show that they need to rely on you and that they are willing to do so, you will have a new sense of your value to them and the potential value of such relationships.

SUMMARY

In this chapter we have discussed the personal benefits to trusting others. In the following chapter we will examine the characteristics of others which lead us to place trust in them. Both of these chapters develop somewhat of a one-sided view favoring trusting others. In the final two chapters we will explore some of the limitations of this practice.

People need others to validate their existence and to lend support to their view of reality. A sense of personal worth is gained from the responses of significant others; failure to gain sought for responses may result in a low self-acceptance, anxiety in communicating with others, and an inability to fully understand one's own psychological make-up. We have noted that a person is a composite of all those significant others with whom he/she interacts. Therefore, an awareness of one's self is proportional to the frequency of interactions with others.

Trust of others is also necessary in order to assure full and undistorted exchange of information. In many situations a person finds him/herself in a mixed motive situation which promotes both competition and cooperation between associates. Cooperative exchange of information may benefit everyone unless one or more persons

KEEP ON TRUSTIN'

decide to withhold or to distort some of their information as a means of gaining a strategic advantage over others. In this case, the competitive choice of behavior may result in a short-term advantage but will probably result in similar behavior from others. This competitive clash of interests may result in a static condition in which any attempt to alter the relationship may result in a significant disadvantage to the cooperative party.

Finally, we have noted that trust of others may be a therapeutically healthy means of reducing the effects of traumatic experiences and establishing more satisfying relationships. By noting those who place trust in us we can risk ourselves in a reciprocal trust, thus reducing inordinate fears of others and gaining more pleasing interpersonal relationships.

Perceptual Bases of Trust

In recent years we have seen two presidents of the United States step down from high office. President Johnson chose not to run for a second term in office. His decision was largely a reflection of loss of trust by the American people in terms of his handling of foreign policy, particularly the war in Vietnam. President Nixon resigned his office in face of congressional distrust of his manner of carrying out his responsibilities.

Most of us can make some general statement about *the degree* to which we are willing to trust another person. When asked why we trust or don't trust someone, often we are not very clear. Why do we trust some people and distrust others? What do we expect of others in order to give them our trust? What do we "see" or perceive that influences our confidence in them?

In our previous chapters we have focused on our personal characteristics which influence us to be (more or less) trusting persons—personality factors that incline us to trust others. In this chapter we will give special attention to perceived characteristics of others that lead us to put our trust in them. In the chapter following this one we will look at situational factors that influence our trust—conditions inherent in various situations that help us trust or distrust.

NATURE OF INTERPERSONAL PERCEPTION

To a large extent, when we "size up" another person, what we see is what we get. By this we mean that if our interpersonal perceptions are inaccurate, limited, or distorted, we will respond to that person *as we perceive him/her* even if this is not the way he/she "really is." For most practical purposes, what we perceive will be that to which we will react. For this reason it is important that we look very carefully at the nature of person perception—those factors that influence the way we "see" people—before we identify the perceived characteristics of others which tend to influence our trust of them.

As we become acquainted with another person we search for clues provided by their behavior, facial expressions, manner of speaking, and general appearance. We note, compare, and weigh all such bits of information as best we can. Generally such an approach works pretty well for us. We tend to become fairly adept at judging status and sometimes beliefs on the basis of mode of dress, physical appearance, and general bearing. By observing behavior in various different situations we make fairly good guesses regarding motives, intentions, and capabilities. Frequently we judge emotional intensity, boldness, aggressiveness, and general dynamism of an individual by his/her facial expressions, posture, and physical actions.

Try as we will, however, frequently we are misled as to attitudes and beliefs of another person. As the motion picture *The Sting* represented, confidence artists frequently adopt modes of dress and ways of speaking in order to mislead their victims. Salesmen, within limited boundaries, often speak or dress to sway the responses of their clients. And most, if not all, of us occasionally dress or behave in ways designed to make a good impression, show off our good points, or achieve a favorable response. Some people are careful in all of this to be true to themselves—their real feelings, beliefs, and backgrounds. Others are not so careful. Because we can be fooled, we have come to recognize that our impressions of others may be inaccurate.

It is even more difficult to be sure of our guesses regarding motives or intentions of others. For example, the teenage son of one of the present writers asked a girl to go with him to a movie. She said she couldn't go. Should he ask her again? He might conclude she isn't as interested in him as he is in her, or he could conclude that her parents don't like him. Or he might conclude she is especially interested in some other boy. As a matter of fact, he later found that she had a date that particular night and that she would like to go to the movies with him on another night!

Most of us have had enough experience in interpersonal relations to know that we should not jump to early conclusions, either favorable or unfavorable, on the basis of little indications of another person's motives or intentions. This learning is reinforced when we discover that various other people in whom we have some confidence form different inferences from some of the same perceived cues. For example, three young men see a young lady at a neighboring restaurant table smile. One suggests she is a warm, kind person simply trying to be friendly to other people. The second man pronounces her a scheming woman looking for someone to buy her lunch. And the third man essentially agrees with the first, but adds "Look out! Her smile wasn't really warm—more cool-friendly and a little bit artificial." When observers disagree on their interpretations of the same behavior, we tend to question our own conclusions and ask how we can know when we are right. Knowing that it is quite possible for us to come to erroneous conclusions, we seek ways of avoiding such errors. One approach is to consider very carefully the process we employ in forming impressions of others, noting carefully the sources of error inherent in this process.

When we meet a person for the first time we quickly form a first impression of him/her. Almost at once we develop a detailed and rather extensive impression from a brief encounter or short conversation; we form early (even if tentative) conclusions regarding personality characteristics, motives, and general background. Solomon Asch was an early researcher of this process and came to this conclusion:

We look at a person and immediately a certain impression of his character forms itself in us . . . Each person confronts us with a large number of diverse characteristics . . . Yet our impression is from the start unified, it is the impression of one person.[1]

Usually these first perceptions heavily influence further interaction with a specific person. Very quickly they are unified into a total impression of the entire person. Such early impressions are surprisingly resistant to change; thus, their effect is more lasting than we ordinarily anticipate. For example, in a study of military officers' first impressions of officer candidates, Cecil Gibb found these initial impressions to be very good predictors of the officers' estimates of these same men three years after the first impressions were formed—all on the basis of a few minutes' interaction.[2]

How do we sift a mass of detailed information so quickly when we observe another person? Even in a brief encounter we note a great number of clues as to what the other person "is like." Sight, sound, sometimes touch, and perhaps smell, all provide us with more data than we can easily assimilate.

To handle such a mass of detail we selectively give special attention to certain types of information. In the first place, we tend to notice what we expect to find.[3] For example, if we are meeting the governor of our state, we note his dignity, friendliness, concern for public problems, and some concern for our own special needs. We are likely pleased to note that he is a real person with a warm, friendly smile and a neatly arranged office. We may easily fail to notice that his hair is cut rather short and that his office chair needs repair. Norman Munn, a well-known psychologist, has described a personal experience that illustrates this point.[4] He kept a colony of white rats in the attic of the psychology building. One afternoon when he went up to look at them he found a number of them outside their cages, dead and partly eaten. He concluded that the damage had been done by wild rats. He went downstairs but shortly returned to the attic. As he was climbing the stairs, he saw, directly in front of the cages, a large wild gray rat! It was standing "tense and trembling." As Munn raised a large glass jar to aim at the rat, he was surprised that it did not move. As he continued to approach "the rat," he found it to be a piece of crumpled grayish paper!

In the second place we sift details quickly by giving special notice to what is of most importance to us at the time; that is, what we have for a mental "set" when we first make a person's acquaintance.[5] Suppose, for example, that you are being interviewed by a prospective supervisor from whom you will be taking orders. You note her way of talking to you, treating you as a human

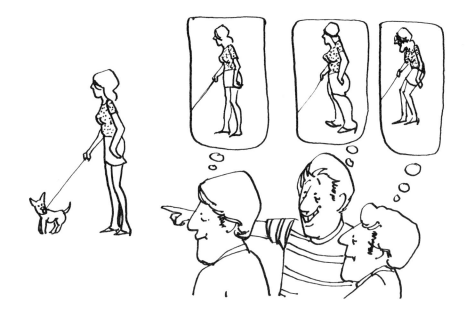

Are all three correct?

being, showing respect for your experience and training, responding to your questions with clarity and sincerity. You are concerned with an estimate of the clarity of requests she may put to you if you are to work for her; you also want to predict the way she will respond to your efforts to follow her instructions. On the other hand, if you were attracted to the same person as a possible date or a special friend, you would pay much more attention to her degree of friendliness, evidence of personal interest in you, and perhaps any indications of her tastes in sports, music, or entertainment.

A third way we filter observed data is to fit it into categories with which we are familiar. Categories with which you are probably quite familiar are athlete, sorority girl, teacher, graduate student, "intellectual," mother, "works part time," married, and "very friendly." The list is almost endless, and, of course, any one person can fit in more than one category. For example, one person could fit *all* the categories. What happens is that we gain some bit of information which calls to mind a category we use, and we conclude he/she is, at least to some extent, that kind of person. This process is called stereotyping; it is useful because it allows us to process incoming data very rapidly; it is of limited value because we pick up some cues and generalize from them, and tend to ignore many cues that might usefully qualify or limit these generalizations. In fitting cues into categories it is dangerous to leap to conclusions. Indeed, many people resent being "typed" so quickly; they feel there is more to them than has been observed.

In the fourth place we tend to see what we *want* to see. Suppose, for example, you have a very good friend who asks you to meet his sister. You will naturally want to like his sister. You meet her; she is neatly dressed, fat, has pretty hair, crooked teeth, looks you in the eye when she speaks, has poor posture, and smiles frequently as you talk to her. You will probably conclude she is a neat, attractive, and friendly person. On the other hand, suppose you have an acquaintance whom you dislike very much; he is dishonest, unpleasant, ugly, and domineering. At a party he comes up to you and insists on introducing his girl friend. She is beautiful! Immediately you suspect she is dumb. You talk to her and perceive solid evidence that she is smart. You now think she may be insincere, even vicious. Later that evening you hear from other friends that she is a very nice person, friendly and sincere. By now, you are convinced that she really isn't the abominable man's special friend—that she really doesn't know him very well! The principle involved has been variously called "balance" or "consistency." Its basic premise is that we like to have the various parts of our world fit together in neat, orderly ways.[6]

If we like a person very much, believe him/her to be sincere, dependable, and intelligent, to hear that he/she is accused of tax fraud produces an unpleasant sense of tension, inconsistency, or imbalance. We seek to reduce this tension in one or more ways: we are selective in our exposure to sources of information (for example, we tend to listen more carefully to friends of the accused person); we derogate (look for reasons for disbelieving) unfriendly sources of information. We probably will be suspicious of persons who accuse our friend of personal aggrandizement, bribery, or status climbing. And we may very quickly forget undesirable evidence against our friend somewhat in the manner of classical cases of amnesia.[7] For example, during the Watergate investigations, some news reporters were called liars by Nixon supporters (and vice versa) and congressional investigators were called "head hunters."

Although the principle of selective attention to information applies in a general way, research has shown that not all people use it; some have a greater ability than others to endure tension caused by inconsistent data regarding their environment.[8] In addition, many people give inconsistent data equivalent attention, showing little or no need to seek out favorable data, derogate unfavorable sources, or forget incongruent facts.[9] It has been said that the most devout readers of Chevrolet brochures are people who have just purchased Chevrolet cars—even (or especially) if the new owner is dissatisfied. Such, of course, is not always the case.

As we look more carefully at perceived characteristics of a person that lead us to trust him/her (in the next section of this chapter) we should keep in mind the limiting factors inherent in the process of perceiving others; we should be aware that we give special attention to cues that are expected, important to us at the time, easily fit into preconceived categories, and are congruent with our prior opinions or viewpoints. In addition, our interpersonal perceptions are limited or distorted by certain factors inherent in interpersonal situations.

In any interpersonal situation we will note some clues about another person early and some late. Perhaps we will see the other person before we hear him/her speak. In any event, there is considerable research evidence that we will be more influenced by data we receive first than by that obtained later—a primacy effect of the order of perceptions.[10] To wit: seeing is believing; but if at first you don't see it, "it" may be hard to believe.

A second situational factor that will influence our perceptions is the degree of believability of the data source. Can we "believe our eyes" (or ears)? We are more readily influenced by information seen first-hand or reported to us by a highly credible source than if we receive the same data second-hand or from less reliable sources.[11]

In recent years researchers have shown considerable interest in the effects of physical attractiveness. Our degree of liking for a person is strongly influenced by the degree of his/her physical beauty as we perceive it.[12] This factor is also very influential upon our overall impression of another person. The results of a rather recent study may serve to illustrate this effect. Dion, Berscheid and Walster had college students look at photographs of three students who had previously been rated by other students as high, average, or low in physical attractiveness.[13] Subjects looked at these photos and then rated the persons in the photos on a number of characteristics (kindness, poise, sincerity, warmth, competitiveness); they also gave estimates of the subjects' future marital happiness, occupational success, and personal overall happiness. Did the level of physical attractiveness of the persons in the photographs influence these other ratings? The results were impressive: persons rated as physically attractive were believed to be more likely to be happily married, more successful in their work and, in general, happier people. Another study, more experiential in nature, involved freshmen students at a computer-date dance at the University of Minnesota.[14] They were randomly paired as dates. Judges rated the physical attractiveness of these students as each purchased a ticket for the dance. Halfway through the dance subjects were asked how well they liked their dates and if future interactions were desired. For both sexes, the more attractive the date (as rated by the judges) the better he/she was liked and the greater the desire for more dates. A number of possible confounding variables were examined for possible influence: grades, intelligence, personality characteristics; however, physical attractiveness was by far of greatest importance. Additional studies of dating preferences have supported these indications of the powerful effect of perceived physical attractiveness on our overall impression of another person.[15] Without quibbling, it can be said that what is thought to be beautiful is perceived as good, ordinarily.

Looking back over the factors described in this section that can restrict, discount, or distort our perception of the cues available to us as we observe another person, one is inclined to wonder how such perceptions are as useful as they are. There is little question that we see one another through filters—rose-colored or otherwise. The cues are filtered, selected, distorted, and collated. Poor as such a process may be, it is still very useful. Indeed, these interpersonal impressions are extremely valuable as we try to relate to one another because, in very practical terms, it's all we have. For example, as you try to work with your instructor you will respond to him/her in terms of this impression; it's all you have to work with as you interact. You may keep your opinions open and flexible knowing the possibility and potential for error in forming such

"How can anyone say she is a thief? How could she be and look so good?"

an impression; however, at the moment, it's all there is and you must choose among your various possible response options (even trying not to respond is a response). In practical terms of interpersonal impression formation, what you see is what you get!

PERCEIVED PERSONAL CHARACTERISTICS INFLUENCING TRUST

We have given special attention to the nature of interpersonal perception because, when a person gains our trust, the characteristics that influence us are not necessarily inherent in that person; rather, they are *perceived* by us as being present. Probably many of the personal characteristics *are* present as perceived; however, as suggested in the prior section, our perceptions may be limited or distorted. We are concerned in this section with the personal characteristics that, when perceived, influence us to trust another person. Essentially, these characteristics concern our estimate of the other person's expertise, character, and potential for action.

Our interest is in all kinds of situations and circumstances in which we might rely upon a person in a risky situation. This approach is much broader than personal characteristics which lead us to believe what somebody tells us—take their word as truth. However, early inquiry into this area was first concerned with the credibility of a

person as a source of information. We shall look at this early interest in source credibility and then broaden our perspective as we look at later investigations of perceived characteristics influencing interpersonal trust.

What do we consider or perceive in another person that makes us believe what he/she tells us? The answer to this question is not entirely clear in specific detail but is generally reliable in broad outline. For a long time it has been of major concern to serious scholars. In his *Rhetoric* Aristotle suggested that *ethos* (a listener's estimation of the believability of a speaker) is based upon three perceived characteristics of the speaker: *intelligence* or correctness of opinions, *character* (primarily honesty), and *good will* or intentions regarding the listener's welfare. Thus, in Aristotle's view, people trust a person as a speaker (that is, a person who may appropriately have influence regarding their attitudes or decisions) in terms of their perceptions of intelligence, honesty, and goodwill.

In 1953 three psychologists, Hovland, Janis and Kelley, renewed the interest of scholars in this question.[16] They were primarily concerned with what we see in a person that gives his "source credibility"—an individual's personal characteristics which help him/her to be effective as a persuasive communicator. After reviewing available information from numerous psychological studies, they concluded that source credibility was the result of (1) the extent to which a communicator is perceived to be a source of valid assertions (his/her "expertness") and (2) the degree of confidence in the communicator's intent to communicate the assertions he/she considers most valid (his/her "trustworthiness"). Hovland and his associates were clearly talking about the perceptual bases of interpersonal trust; they combined Aristotle's factors of perceived character and goodwill under the single concept of "trustworthiness"—perceived intention to be a reliable communicator. However, in another section of this same review they did give special attention to the perception of a speaker's intentions as having influence on a listener's estimate of his/her credibility.[17]

Since 1953 additional research on the factors influencing source credibility have added to our knowledge.[18] Most of these factor analytical studies disagree to some extent with the Hovland, Janis, and Kelley model of perceived factors of credibility. Trustworthiness is not a simple, intent-oriented factor according to other investigators. Anderson investigated the credibility of well-known persons.[19] He found a major factor covering honesty, morality, fairness, and goodness—mainly items that referred to a source's character; this factor he labelled "evaluation." He also found a second factor involving strength, swiftness, aggressiveness and activity; this factor he labeled "dynamism."

Public speakers studied by communication researchers Berlo, Lemert and Mertz were perceived as being credible in terms of three factors: (1) "qualifications," a factor essentially concerned with the speaker's expertise; (2) "safety," a factor very similar to Hovland's concept of trustworthiness; and (3) "dynamism," a factor very much like Anderson's second factor, similarly labelled.[20]

In a study of responses to speaker introductions (not the speakers *per se*) McCroskey found that two very strong factors emerged: "authoritativeness" (very similar to the previously identified factor of expertness,) and "character" (much like Berlo's safety).[21]

In looking over these studies of perceived factors that influence source credibility of public speakers, there appears to be little question that two factors, expertness and reliability, are influential. In a lesser way, perhaps with some speakers on some topics, perceived dynamism of the speaker may exert some influence.

At least two research efforts have attempted to study the perceptual bases of trust on a much broader basis than the perceived characteristics of a public speaker. Schweitzer and Ginsburg asked subjects to pick credible persons from among their acquaintances and to list the characteristics that influenced their belief in what such a person said.[22] In addition, these subjects identified significant credibility factors involved in high credibility and low credibility introductions of public speakers. Factor analysis of these data identified eleven factors. The two major ones

were very broad, identified by these researchers as (1) trustworthiness, and (2) expertise.[23] However, the major conclusion of this study is that characteristics other than the two listed above are significant in influencing perceived trustworthiness in various communication situations.

A factor analytical study by Giffin was designed to identify perceived characteristics of trusted persons in groups; concern here was much broader than for factors influencing credibility solely as a communication source.[24] All factors thought to have any influence on interpersonal trust were analyzed. This study indicated that trust is influenced by perceptions of the following:

1. *Expertness*—this may be in terms of quantity of relevant information, degree of ability or skill, or validity of judgment.

2. *Reliability*—a characteristic perceived as dependability, predictability, or favorable intent of the trusted person.

3. *Dynamism*—behavior perceived as more active than passive, and more open or frank than closed or deceptive.

These three factors appear to be the primary characteristics that others perceive and consider as they decide the degree to which a person can be trusted as a member of a group.[25]

For our purpose of describing the perceived bases of trust it is appropriate to present a detailed description of the three personal characteristics that have arisen in study after study of factors that influence credibility and trust: reliability, expertness, and dynamism.

Old reliable at the wheel

Reliability

In a number of studies this perceived characteristic appeared to be the most important of the three. The reliability factor is broad in scope and includes perceptions of honesty, sincerity, goodness, morality, kindness, and patience. In part, these elements reflect perceived willingness to consider others; reliability includes predictability of behavior that is favorably oriented toward the trusting person. The essence of the reliability factor involves the trusting person's concepts of morality and justice.[26]

Predictability of the behavior of a person whom you might trust involves your judgment of his/her intentions, especially those that might affect your goals or ambitions. In theory, at least, it could be argued that a person's behavior might be very predictable, but that this behavior would have a negative influence on your goals or desired circumstances. For example, you may be of the opinion that the behavior of the governor of your state is very predictable, but will be damaging to goals inherent in your political philosophy. Does predictability, as such, lead to trust? There is some slight evidence that this is true.[27] However, for the most part, people do not appear to perceive a person as reliable whose behavior is predictably hostile to their own goals or desired circumstances. Only if the trusted person's intentions are predictably friendly toward such goals are they perceived as reliable.

Expertness

In all studies of perceived personal characteristics influencing credibility or trust this factor has been significant. It is a broad concept involving knowledge, intelligence, experience, education, training, being informed and logical, and excellent in judgments. Of course, in each particular case where an individual decides to trust another, knowledge or experience that is relevant to the existing conditions is of special importance.[28] It is quite clear that the essence of this factor is perceived relevant wisdom.

Dynamism

This perceived characteristic seems to be of somewhat less importance than the other two. In some studies it seems to collapse into the factor of reliability, perhaps because in some way a situation is suggested in which an active person is viewed as more dependable. In other studies it does not appear to be significant.

The concept of dynamism in studies where it has been shown significant involves perceived strength, swiftness, aggressiveness, boldness, decisiveness, and perceptions of a person as energetic, frank, open, colorful, and extroverted. The essence of this factor appears to be open, frank activeness.

The available evidence suggests that perceived dynamism is more significant in determining one's willingness to trust others in real-life situations and of less importance in students' responses to introductions of speakers not actually presented to the respondents.[29]

Personal characteristics such as reliability, expertness, and dynamism may be viewed as personality traits or qualities. In forming an estimate of a person such characteristics are usually thought of as enduring, paramount, and significant. When we are interested in assessing such traits, we usually infer the degree of their presence by observing a person's actions.[30] We notice that people do certain things. As we watch these behaviors, we generalize to personality characteristics, motives, or intentions. For example, we notice that a classmate comes to class on time for a week and we conclude that person is dependable. Watching a person's behavior and attributing to that person a trait, motive, or intention, is called by scholars the "attribution process" in impression formation.[31]

Assessing a Person's Reliability

In assessing reliability, expertness, and dynamism we tend to use a few special techniques or procedures. In part, we tend to watch for certain behaviors. As we form an impression of a person's reliability, we tend to pay special attention to possible deceit. For example, do people do what they say they will do? Do they say things they don't mean and later "take them back" (or try to)? Do they refuse to give clear answers to relevant questions? At different times are their actions clearly inconsistent?

Very often we must decide whether or not a person's acts truly reflect his/her intentions or if such actions are designed to deceive us. We are quite aware that people can disguise their true feelings and attitudes. Even so, our general experience demonstrates that we can, many times, guess the true intentions of others by noting carefully their behavior. To a large extent we can recognize their motives and determine what they are trying to do. How we are able to do this is not entirely clear, but two social psychologists who have specialized in this area offer a suggestion. Edward Jones and Keith Davis surveyed existing research and theory, deriving this tentative conclusion: we manage to move rather effectively from observations of overt behavior to guesses about a person's intentions by focusing upon two specific aspects of his or her behavior.[32]

We pay particular attention to actions that could have had only *one or at most only a very few motivations.* For example, suppose that you are asked to work with a man who has just married a woman who is very pretty, extremely bright, and very wealthy. The act of marriage in this case tells you little about the character of the man with whom you will work. But suppose, instead, that when you met this man's wife you discovered her to be unattractive, gross, stupid, mean-tempered, but very rich. You immediately guess at her husband's motives as well as possible attitudes that might affect your relationship with him. In addition, you start to form an opinion about his character.

Second, Jones and Davis suggest that we tend to focus upon acts of others that are *inconsistent with generally accepted social norms of behavior.* Suppose, for example, you are quite friendly with one of your classmates who comes to class on time and does his work like most of the other class members. Then, one day he appears in class wearing a university team track suit. Immediately you start making inferences about his possible problem of meeting the requirements of this class and keeping up with his track training. You also begin to make additional inferences about his motivations, intentions, determination and persistence, as well as about his attitudes toward customs or norms of dress and appearance. Thus, we tend to pay special attention to deviant behavior as we assess the motives and intentions of others from observations of their actions.

A third area of behavior not mentioned by Jones and Davis, but one that may be very valuable in assessing the reliability of a person, is that of *private behavior.* Behavior in public may be quite convincing until a person's behavior in private disconfirms it. For example, people holding extreme political views may refrain from voicing them in public, letting passive acceptance of "normal" views of others help them avoid criticism or attack. If, however, private acts, such as the famous or infamous "Nixon Tapes," are different from public behavior, they are often viewed as a more dependable index of a person's true intentions or motives.[33] We are often tempted to "eavesdrop" on persons whose intentions are very important to us; likewise, the private behavior of public officials often becomes the target of "bugging" and other electronic devices. By obtaining such information about their private actions, a more valid assessment of a person's character is thought to be possible.

A fourth consideration in the assessment of a person's reliability is the attribution of *causes* of his or her behavior. Guesses about the reliability of a person involve conclusions about his/her intentions and/or motives. In drawing these conclusions one of the first questions to be faced is the degree to which a person performed an act of his/her own volition; that is, *chose* to behave in a certain way or was *forced* to do so by outside or environmental pressures. Were optional choices of behavior available—and were they recognized as such? Or was a certain way of behaving the only choice left open at that time for that individual? For example, a student may elect to take Economics 240. She may choose to do so from a number of possible options. Suppose, later, she drops the course. Did she so choose? Or was she forced to drop because of lack of appropriate prerequisite courses? Perhaps she was hospitalized with a long-term illness and could not keep up with the class requirements.

The determination of the extent to which a person's action is of his/her own volition or behavior coerced by external forces is a very important one in assessing his/her intentions or motivations. If an act is truly the only option a person has, little can be inferred from it regarding character, reliability, motives, or intent. A number of scholars have studied this problem; however, the most compelling analysis is provided by Harold H. Kelley.[34] Kelley has suggested that we may conclude a person's actions are the result of his/her own volition if they are (1) deviant from the way other persons act; (2) consistent on specific similar occasions; and (3) deviant from the way this person acts in other somewhat similar situations. For example, suppose a student acts very hostilely toward a teacher whom other students treat in a friendly, cooperative manner; this student also acts hostilely *every time* he/she meets this teacher; in addition, this student treats his/her other teachers in a friendly, cooperative manner. According to Kelley, we could conclude that this student is motivated by *internal* forces to treat this teacher in a hostile way. On the other hand, if another student treats this teacher about the same way he/she treats other teachers, is sometimes rather friendly, and at others fairly cool, and tends to treat all his/her teachers in about this same varied manner, little could be inferred about internal motivations from such responses. We would tend to look for external forces to account for such varied behavior.[35]

As a passing comment on this problem of determining whether external or internal forces are the cause of a person's action, we are prone to assign internal causes whenever possible—even if unreasonable. Recent investigations tend to show that in terms of helping our image in the eyes of others, it really does little good to say we are sorry when we have made a mistake. Even if it was an accident and no fault of our own, we are viewed somehow as having allowed the accident to happen and thus must take some blame for it.[36]

In assessing the reliability of a person there is a special problem involving his or her communication: it involves honesty or sincerity. Do statements a person makes reflect his/her true feelings, motive, or intentions? Most people's ability to engage in hypocrisy is truly remarkable—even to the extent of occasionally fooling themselves. However, in spite of the ability of most people to engage in flattery, exaggeration, deception, and dishonesty, we are surprisingly capable of separating sincerity from deceit. We are able to do this by employing essentially three criteria: (1) is the statement generally different from what we would expect most people to make, especially if the statement risks scorn, derision or censure—for example, a strong support for the so-called Watergate activity;[37] (2) does the statement deviate markedly from neutrality; that is, does it tend to take an extreme position—for example, a strong indictment of existing American foreign policy;[38] (3) is it unlikely that the person can profit from making the statement; that is, does it seem to have little value as support for his/her vested interest—for example, an official of the Chamber of Commerce would have little to gain personally by condemning illicit practices of certain businessmen.[39]

In general, the assessment of a person's reliability by observing his/her acts and statements is a very complex operation. Few of us assess in a systematic, deliberate fashion—we tend to look and listen and follow our feelings or intuition. The material presented here may be useful in two ways: we may monitor our own reliability; and we may check our estimates of the reliability of others by more careful application of procedures suggested in this section.

Assessing a Person's Expertness

At first glance it may appear that forming an opinion of a person's expertness is a simple task. Let's look very carefully. In the first place, we must base our estimate primarily on what he or she does, not self-proclaimed capability. So we must look at actions that successfully accomplish some identifiable goal (even if it is verbal activity, such as feats of memory).

Success and achievement may be the results of more than one factor: (1) a person's level of ability or expertness; (2) the amount of effort expended; (3) the difficulty of the task; and (4) the role of luck or chance.[40] The assessment of task difficulty can generally be achieved by observing attempts of various persons to accomplish the same or a similar task. An estimate of the part played by luck or chance can be derived in about

the same way. Neither of these factors is beyond our ability to estimate if we can obtain information on how other people perform in similar situations; this is possible on many tasks but not on some—such as fighting a military battle or surviving a tornado. When replication of situations is costly or impossible, we have learned to use simulated experiences which "come close."

Calculation of effort expended is somewhat difficult. Two approaches have been used: (1) the size of the incentives in the situation—the greater the obtainable rewards, the greater the effort inferred; and (2) various expressive signs of effort involved, such as perspiring, showing tension, and degree of apparent concentration. Neither of these approaches is very certain; taken together, they provide only a fairly probable estimate of effort involved.

Without some estimate of these three factors—effort, task difficulty, and luck—no fair estimate of a person's ability can be formed by observing his/her degree of success in achievement or performing tasks. But when these estimates are made, a person's ability or expertness can be inferred in fairly straightforward manner—then success in achieving is a sign of knowledge, intelligence, skill, or some combination of these that can help a person be viewed as expert in some specific way.

In forming estimates of a person's ability we apparently tend to give the individual "the benefit of the doubt." That is, if a person tends to succeed, we ordinarily attribute his/her success to ability and effort; if, on the other hand, a person seems to be dogged by failure, we tend to attribute lack of success to environmental factors beyond his/her control—bad luck, perhaps, in the sense that he/she was handed a tough task, a rough situation, or got off to a "bad start."[41]

Once we have attributed a given level of expertise to a person it appears very difficult to alter this estimate even in the face of new, contrary evidence. Recent experiments show that new evidence that stands in contradiction to our earlier estimates will be explained away on the basis of "he/she tried harder" (put forth greater effort) or had a run of good luck—rather than be accepted as the basis for a revised estimate of the person's ability.[42] This finding appears to have rather unsettling implications for the benefits of education, training, or one's personal efforts for improvement or change. It reminds us of the biblical statement (made originally in a different sense): "To him who hath shall be given, and from him who hath not, shall be taken away." To keep such undesirable practices from happening by default, perhaps we should admonish one another to make more careful estimates of people's ability,

"ED, I THOUGHT YOU SAID THIS WAS ONE GIANT STEP FOR MANKIND!"

making appropriate allowances for possible change. This is especially important in the case of the individual who tries, without benefit of formal schooling or training, to improve his/her own expertise. It is indeed unfortunate if we ignore change in others as a result of formal training, but at least going to school or participating in a training program shows they are trying. In any case, actual changes in an individual's ability should be reflected in changed estimates of expertise by his/her associates.

Assessing a Person's Dynamism

To our knowledge very little careful investigation has been made of the ways in which we form an opinion of a person's activeness, frankness or openness to others. So far as we know dynamism is assessed in a rather straightforward manner, by observing directly a person's behavior and deriving a general impression of this factor.

Research on observable behaviors that contribute to an impression of *openness* has been begun,[43] but needs to be carried further before we can offer a summarizing statement regarding dynamism as a factor in impression formation.

SUMMARY

We have explored in some depth those characteristics of a person that appear to influence the degree of trust placed in him/her by others. The process of perceiving another person influences this degree of personal trust; we have indicated that we tend to perceive what we expect, what is important to us, and what we want to see. We tend to fit data into preconceived categories, interpreting new data to fit with old. We hold to early impressions. We are especially influenced by impressions of personal attractiveness; very often what we perceive as beautiful is also perceived as good.

Perceived personal characteristics that appear to influence personal trust were identified as reliability, expertness, and dynamism.

In assessing a person's reliability we tend to note actions having only one possible motive, actions inconsistent with social norms, and a person's private behavior, especially if it is inconsistent with public behavior. We make guesses about the possible causes of actions observed, and pay special attention to signs of insincerity.

In assessing the expertness of an individual we note successful achievements of various kinds. We carefully consider the possible influence of effort, task difficulty, and luck in succeeding in various achievements as we form an impression of a person's ability. Most people are not very careful to take appropriate notice of increased expertness once an early opinion has been formed.

The study of assessment of a person's dynamism has received little careful attention. Exploratory studies of perceived openness as an influence on interpersonal trust deserve much further work.

Situational Factors Influencing Trust

In the previous chapter we concentrated upon characteristics of a person that, when perceived, may influence us to trust him or her. In the present chapter we will focus on environmental variables that, in a given situation, influence a person to trust another. As we observe the relative degree of one or another of these situational factors, we compare our potential gain from trusting with the probable risk of our trust being violated. Thus, in conjunction with our individual personality characteristics that make it easy or hard for us to trust another, along with our perceptions of the relevant characteristics of the other person, we consider situational factors that show high or low probability of gain versus risk. In this fashion we arrive at a decision of trust—or not to trust.

As we grow and develop we observe popular practice in trusting behavior; in this sense, society provides us with guidelines regarding situations in which we should be willing to trust one another. Second, as two or more individuals interact, they develop interpersonal expectations which lead them to trust one another in certain circumstances. Third, the perceived probability of achieving the outcome requiring us to trust another person will vary from situation to situation. And fourth, the perceived probability of the trusted person's violation of our trust is an additional situational factor influencing our decision. Each of these four factors will be discussed in this chapter. Together, they can be considered as situational variables influencing the trust of one person by another.

SITUATIONAL GUIDELINES

Suppose you would like to be a banker. The old saying used to be, "Anybody can be a banker; all it takes is money." In modern times, of course, we know this saying doesn't hold. Popular practice, including state and federal statutes, provide stiff penalties for bankers who violate the trust of their clients. In a much less strict way we generally hold accountable persons who agree to function as automobile mechanics, baby-sitters, television salesmen, and school teachers within limits set by society. You can expect persons to honor your trust in ways commensurate with their titles or labels. Common practice of manufacturers and retailers of name brand merchandise is to allow their clients to hold them responsible for claims made—at least within reasonable limits. Legal sanctions often help to encourage such responsibility.[1]

For each specific situation allowances are often made for individual ways of seeing things or behaving. Thus, lawyers may choose to use one or another witness in a court case, but such idiosyncratic choices are allowed only within reasonable boundaries or a judge may declare a mistrial and another attempt will be made to achieve justice.

For most common situations such as selling property, making a contract, repairing a house, and even sailing a boat, common practice has provided guidelines for us in trusting one another. Many of these behaviors are required by law with appropriate provision of penalties for violators, such as loss of money already paid when breaking a lease.

The rules for such various situations are rather numerous and specific as well as subject to change or modification in certain localities (such as "Smoking Permitted Only in the Lobby"). We learn many of them as we grow, later as we interact, and even more as we travel. Our point here is that they exist and directly influence us as we decide to trust one another in specific situations or transactions.

INTERPERSONAL EXPECTATIONS

In the previous chapter we suggested that as two people interact a situation may occur wherein one will have occasion to rely upon the other. When such an occasion arises, the person to be relied upon or trusted will be assessed in terms of reliability, expertness, and dynamism. However, in some small ways, each new trusting situation is different, and at any time the relationship between the two people may be different.

As a relationship is formed and developed by two persons, the relationship itself will be defined by each of them, and then later, redefined. For many relationships, common practice has set certain boundaries and within these boundaries prescribed certain behaviors. For example, when a military officer and a private meet, they are expected to exchange salutes. Society tends to enforce these behaviors once the relationship has been agreed upon by the individual participants and announced to the world.

Within the confines of such behavioral boundaries, one of the persons in the relationship can depend upon the other to behave in certain trustworthy ways. For example, as a man and a woman meet and form a strong, personal relationship, society's requirement of specific behavior is within very wide boundaries, mainly requirements of courtesy and friendliness. However, when this couple marry and announce it to the world, narrower boundaries and more specific behaviors are expected by society and even supported by legal sanctions; for example, payment of each other's debts. In special ways, the members of this marriage partnership can count on each other, more or less. Even so, as they continue to interact, the behavior of each is observed by the other, and the finer points of the interpersonal relations are identified and defined. For example, can they count on each other for evidence of affection—not too little nor too much? How much domination by one of them over the other will be sought? And will be accepted?[2]

In a relationship, perceptions of each other's behavior make possible "fine tuning" of the anticipated behaviors. Each person is constantly shifting perspectives from his/her own position to that of the other, "vicariously oscillating" in a process that gives each of them a clearer understanding of what he/she can expect from the other in given situations.[3]

Interpersonal perceptions, of course, are not perfect as we have suggested. We tend to see each other too much as we want to and not enough as we really are. Expected behavior in a relationship is only probable, not certain.[4] Even so, expected behavior in a relationship provides a useful basis for personal trust. In particular, it gives the persons involved more precise knowledge of what to expect from each other in specific situations.

PERCEIVED PROBABILITY OF DESIRED OUTCOME

You and I will trust someone in a given situation only if we think there is some possibility of our achieving our desired outcome. In considering the probability of achieving our goal in comparison with the probability of our trust being violated, it may be useful to use a special set of symbols. Let G stand for *gain* and L stand for *loss* (or violation of our trust). In addition let (p) stand for comparative probability.

Consider a situation where the potential loss is greater than the potential gain, with loss highly probable, such as taking an airplane ride with an inexperienced pilot in a thunderstorm. If "ride" is the only desirable factor possible in this situation, most of us would feel that the potential loss is much greater than the potential gain, and if the pilot has very little chance of flying (and again landing) the plane in such a storm, we could describe the situation as L over G, with L probable, thus $\frac{L(p)}{G}$. If we chose to put ourselves into this situation, we would not be "trusting" the pilot. Rather, we would be viewed as stupid, gullible, or crazy.[5]

Now let us consider another kind of situation in which the potential gain is greater than the potential loss, such as buying a lottery ticket for a dollar on the chance (very, very low probability) that the drawing will give us the prize of a million dollars. Such a situation may be described as $\frac{G}{L(p)}$ and is not generally viewed as trusting but
gambling or "taking a chance on a long shot."

Let us suppose a situation in which the potential gain is greater than the potential loss, with the gain very probable if we put ourselves in that situation; for example, getting up and going to work tomorrow with the expectation that our employer will pay us for it. This kind of situation can be described as $\frac{G(p)}{L}$ and is probably the most common kind of a situation we meet throughout our lives. There is little risk involved, and such a situation is not ordinarily thought of as a trusting one. Perhaps we could say that we are trusting our employer to pay us, but if we have always been paid on time before and have no reason to become suspicious this time (that is, if the probability of gain is high) we are not trusting in the ordinary sense—at least, not very much.

The true trusting situation is one in which the potential loss is greater than the potential gain, with gain more likely or probable than loss. Suppose, for example, a mother wants to go to a high school play in which her daughter is performing and needs a baby-sitter for her one-year-old child. Here the potential loss is great—it could involve even the life of the baby—and the potential gain is relatively small but highly probable. This situation can be described as $\frac{L}{G(p)}$, and is a true trusting situation . She trusts the sitter to take care of her baby, and gains the reward of attending the play.

Inherent, of course, in such a trusting situation is the mother's perception of the value of potential gain to be achieved as well as her perception of the probability that the sitter will take good care of her child. In such a situation, if the only sitter available is a seven-year-old boy, known generally to be quite undependable, and if the mother perceives the situation as we have described it, the (p) has changed from $\frac{L}{G(p)}$ to $\frac{L(p)}{G}$ and she is not likely to exercise such "stupidity."

In our lives various kinds of situations are constantly appearing, changing, and reappearing with new L and G configurations. In order for us to trust another person, the situation in which we

"LOOK AT IT THIS WAY JOE. I HAVE MORE TO GAIN THAN YOU HAVE TO LOSE!"

will trust him/her must be perceived as having this form: $\frac{L}{\overline{G}(p)}$.

Certain kinds of situations are often set up with special ground rules. For example, in playing cards, you might have a strong overriding motive to beat one of the other players. This "motivational orientation" would be based upon your perception of the particular situation, and the desire to win over a particular person would have a strong influence on how you play the game.[6] Morton Deutsch, a social psychologist and an early researcher in this field, has called this orientation "competitive." In such a situation you will likely trust no one. You may act as if you are trusting in order to maneuver your opponent into a condition so that you can then beat him/her, but you will not be likely to trust other players in any realistic sense.

A second common kind of situation is one in which your motivation will be to achieve your own personal goal without concern for beating anybody. At the same time you may enter such a situation without any desire to help anybody. This is the kind of situation frequently found in the business world where businessmen are, in their view, simply striving to do well or make a profit; not exactly winning over anybody; just being successful in their chosen work. Many professional people such as lawyers and doctors have this orientation. In situations where you hold this personal achievement orientation (called "individualistic" by Deutsch[7]), whether or not you decide to trust the other person will depend upon the perceptual and situation variables we have described earlier. In particular, if you can talk to the person, and if he/she convinces you that your trust will not be violated, then you are fairly likely to go ahead and trust.[8] As a matter of fact, however, such communication and promised reliability actually changes the situation, and ordinarily puts it into more of a cooperative mode.

A third motivational orientation is one of cooperation. With such an orientation, you will feel that the welfare of the person to be trusted is of concern to you as well as your own welfare, and that the other person feels the same way. In such fashion working partnerships and marriages are formed, and over time, mutual trust may develop, grow, and flourish.

As you enter any given situation it might be useful to check your own personal motives—your motivational orientation. Is it to beat some particular other person? Is it to achieve personal gain without any concern for beating someone and also without any particular concern for helping anyone? Or is your basic motivation one in which you are concerned about the goals of the other person as much as you are your own, with full

confidence that they feel the same way? Probably only the latter case will warrant your full trust.

PERCEIVED PROBABILITY OF TRUST VIOLATION

In any given situation where we might consider trusting a person, the degree of "risk" is an important factor—in many cases, the controlling one. Here we are primarily concerned with whether or not that person in that situation will violate the trust we place in him/her.

Six different variables will warrant your concern: possibility of gain by trusted person if he/she violates your trust; your power over the truster; evidence that the trusted person trusts you; trust placed by other people in the person you are going to trust; promises made to you by that person; and the possible presence of an external threat to both of you. Each of these variables will be discussed in terms of their influence on your perception of the probability that your trust might be violated.

Possibility of Gain by Trust Violation

Suppose a woman asks you to hold her baby while she purchases an airline ticket. Do you have much to gain by violating her trust? Probably not; you are waiting for a plane departure and you can't do much else profitably with your time. If she knows this, she will be more apt to trust you with her child than if she thought you might profit from a kidnapping. Incidentally, rich people have a hard time trusting anybody because they have so much to lose in so many ways.

In a rather elaborate experimental study, Solomon studied the influence of possible gain by trust violation.[9] He had subjects play games for money in which they could try to beat one another, seek to maximize their own money rewards without concern for others, or cooperate to win as much as possible for both players. He found that the greater the potential gain by trust violation, the less likely were his subjects to trust each other. A follow-up study found the same general results.[10] This was especially true when trust was violated and loss was great. It took a long time for the trust violator to regain the confidence of the person who had been "let down." This research also demonstrated that the greatest amount of trust is generated when trust is never violated, but that once let down, we seldom want to trust that person again.[11]

Power over the Trusted Person

Suppose your younger brother is just learning to drive a car. Quite possibly he will receive instruction and experience in a car specially equipped with dual controls. He will be trusted with control of the car within limits; specifically, the control can be taken over by the instructor at any time. Many parents with children learning to drive have wished for such a car, particularly at times when it appeared that trust in the young drivers was unjustified.

In an experimental study where subjects played games for money, Solomon varied the ability of one player to control the behavior of another; he found that the greater a person's power over another, the more likely he/she was to trust that other person.[12] Although it is risky to generalize from game-playing to everyday human interaction, the findings of these gaming studies seem to confirm our casual observations of trusting behavior.[13]

In a similar game-playing experimental study, Evans attempted to determine the effect of a promise.[14] Subjects asked their opposites in the game to give a promise that trust placed in them (purportedly in an attempt to achieve cooperative benefits for both players) would not be violated; if trust were violated, the violator would be penalized by having a certain number of points subtracted from his/her score. Evans' results showed that gaining such a promise significantly increased the cooperative behavior of subjects. Apparently, according to Evans, this increased reliance on the promised behavior was based on an attitude of trust.[15] A recent study by Kruglanski looked at the behavior of supervisors and employees in an attempt to study people in real-life situations rather than the artificial setting of game playing.[16] Kruglanski found that supervisors were more willing to trust their employees when external influences on trust violation could be controlled.

Evidence that Trusted Person Trusts You

A third situational variable that can influence your trust in a person is some credible indication that he/she trusts you. In practical terms, such a situation is one in which the trusted person is actively relying upon you and will suffer some undesired consequence if you violate his/her trust. In effect, you have some control over his/her trust violation by retaliating with similar violation. Sometimes this condition is called mutual trust or interdependency.

A recent study by Dale Leathers used subjects in an experiment in which interdependence was promoted.[17] Confederates of the experimenter demonstrated quite clearly that personal trust of the subjects was gained when confederates trusted them, expected this trust to be honored in return, promised retaliatory trust violation if expected trust was violated, made an enforceable promise to the subjects that they (the confederates) would not violate their trust, and did all this in the presence of a third person who posed some degree of threat to both of them. Leathers' results essentially demonstrated the principle that when we see other people trusting us, we tend to trust them more. In the latter part of the experiment, the confederates violated the trust placed in them by the subjects, who then rapidly proceeded to withdraw their trust.

Others' Trust in the Person You Trust

We tend to trust people in situations where we see that other people trust them. Such behavior is easily visible in politics, business, small groups, and most interpersonal relations. This process is an application of a broader principle sometimes called the "conformity" principle, wherein we tend to do what we see others doing even if, at times, we can't always see the sense of it.

A long series of studies of social conformity influence started with this question: will persons believe what others tell them if these others agree, *even when contrary evidence is clearly before their eyes?*[18] These studies have clearly demonstrated that we tend to distrust our own senses when three or more others agree on reports of perceptions that disagree with our own. Clearly, interpersonal trust is involved in this process, and we tend to trust persons who are trusted by others, even if they disagree with us, at least in some minor ways.[19]

Promises by Person to Be Trusted

We have indicated earlier that an enforceable promise—that is, a promise under conditions where we can apply sanctions or retaliate if the promise is broken—will increase our tendency to trust a person. What about the effect of a promise under conditions where we cannot retaliate if it is broken? Do we tend to trust people more just because they promise us they can be trusted?

Part of the study by Evans investigated the effect of unenforceable promises on trusting behavior.[20] Rather surprisingly, at least within the confines of experimental game-playing, the influence of an unenforceable promise was almost the same as that of an enforceable promise, in terms of perceiving another person as trustworthy. However, apparently the interpersonal attitudes were not quite the same, for when subjects were asked to adopt trusting behavior regarding the promising person, there were significant differences in the behaviors adopted toward those who gave enforceable promises in comparison with those who gave unenforceable ones. Apparently we like to say we trust people who promise us that they can be trusted; but when it comes to "putting our money where our mouth is," we are apt to be more receptive to those whose promises are backed by opportunity for us to retaliate if the promise is broken.

Presence of External Threat

A sixth situational factor that can increase our tendency to trust a person is the presence of an external threat. Suppose, for example, your employer becomes angry at you on some unreasonable basis. Perhaps he/she blames you for an error that was really his/her fault. You will likely look around among the other employees to see whom you might talk with—ask advice, obtain correct information, and so forth. Your willingness to trust such a fellow-worker will likely increase as you feel the pressure of the situation rising. Casual observation of common experience has shown that we tend to trust people more when we need them than when we don't.

Now suppose that the employer unjustly blames two of you for his/her mistake. Here is a situation that could be called "mutual opposition," or a threat from a third party. James Farr, a social psychologist, hypothesized that under such a condition, mutual trust would be increased significantly.[21] In his experimental study of game-playing, he paired his subjects and then introduced a threatening third person for each pair. As predicted, the trusting (cooperative) behavior of the threatened pair significantly increased. Common experience of generations of people has produced the saying that we tend to join hands in the face of a common enemy. Apparently the line of reasoning involved is that, in the face of a common threat, the person you are trusting is less likely to violate your trust because, as he/she also is relying on you, he/she is equally vulnerable.

In practical terms, you might keep in mind your potential need to trust someone if it appears that, at some time, the going might get tough. Many married couples have been surprised to find that the heat of a minor quarrel faded to practically zero in a situation where one of their children suddenly became ill with a temperature of one hundred and three degrees. Such a situation calls for cooperation and, within reasonable limits, mutual trust.

ASSESSMENT OF PROBABILITY OF GAIN VERSUS LOSS

Each of the situational variables we have discussed can have impact on our decisions to trust one another. In any given situation we consider the potential effect of each of them and intuitively do some mental arithmetic. We assess the likelihood that we will gain the objective that requires us to rely upon another person. We also arrive at some conception of the likelihood that our trust may be violated. We compare the two degrees of probability, and depending upon how strongly we desire to achieve our objective, we arrive at a decision. Sometimes all these mental gymnastics are performed subconsciously, and without knowing exactly why, we know what we are going to do. In any case, to the extent that we actually realize what we are doing, comparison of probability of loss with probability of gain is the basis for arriving at our decision.

SUMMARY

In this chapter we have described situational factors that can influence our decisions to trust one another. We have suggested that, for many situations, common practice of society has provided guidelines for trusting behavior, such as reliance upon a person to live up to the terms of a contract or sale. For many such situations specific behaviors are required by legal statutes, with penalties provided for violations.

We have also suggested that in any given interpersonal relationship, interpersonal expectations of behavior are developed as the relationship grows and thrives. In such situations we come to learn more and more clearly how much and for what we can depend upon one another.

In any given situation the probability of your gaining a desired outcome by trusting another person will vary. In some cases this probability may be almost "for certain"; in others, it may be probable only to a slight degree—a "long shot." For us to exercise trust, the probability of gain must be greater than the probability of loss; otherwise, we will be gambling or just taking a chance on achieving our desired end. How we perceive this probability may be influenced by our attitude toward any given situation: Is it a "game" in which our objective should be to beat the other person no matter what it costs us? Is it routine business in which we should try to do our best for ourselves without concern for benefit or harm to others? Or is it a situation in which we really ought to be cooperative, seeking the greatest benefit *for us and others,* with reason to believe that the others involved have the same cooperative attitude? Only this third approach is likely to draw a high degree of trust and reliance upon another.

We have described six situational factors that may influence our perception of the probability that the trust we place in a person may be violated: possibility of gain by the trust violator, power over him/her, evidence that he/she is relying on us,

trust by other people in the trusted person, promises made to us by him/her, and presence of a threatening third person or other external source of danger. Each of these factors can influence our perception of the degree of risk that our trust might be violated.

In any given situation we determine as best we can the likelihood that, by trusting a person, we can gain a desired outcome; in addition, we determine the likelihood that our trust will be violated. We compare the two probabilities, and if the balance lies on the side of probability that we will achieve our objective in that particular situation, we will tend to extend our trust.

The Ethics of Personal Trust

In recent years we have heard many people advocate increased cooperation between individuals, groups, races, and nations. Implied in such suggestions is the notion that we should learn to trust each other more. Along with such emphasis on cooperation is an implicit suggestion that competition is bad and ought to be avoided.

It is often suggested that many of the conflict problems of the world—interpersonal, interracial, and international—would be resolved if we would just trust one another. Should we try to trust each other more? In this chapter we are less concerned with a discussion of conditions that promote trust or conditions that trust affects. We turn our attention to a question of personal ethics: what should we do about trusting others or having them trust us?

RECENT CULTURAL EMPHASES ON TRUST

During the past decade we have seen the development of a strong emphasis on people's need to establish warm interpersonal relationships. This has been particularly true in America and Europe. Perhaps this emphasis has been most visible in the workshops, institutes, and conferences of what has sometimes been called the Human Potential Movement. In most such cases the objective has been to help individuals realize their full potential for developing more satisfying human relationships. T-Groups, encounter groups, and human relations workshops have heen held in scores of cities. This movement has been stimulated by the studies and essays of Carl Rogers, Abraham Maslow, Warren Bennis, Matthew Miles, Leland Bradford, and a host of other students of humanistic psychology. One reflection of this emphasis has been the growth of courses in interpersonal communication and human relations on many college campuses.

Most of the writers in this movement agree that, for the development of a warm personal relationship, a requisite condition is a climate of trust.[1] In order for us to relate well to others, we must, in some way, reduce our defensiveness, deception, and avoidance behaviors. The optimally desired condition is that of mutual trust—two (or more) people trusting one another. Some scholars like Rensis Likert[2] argue that only by increasing our trust and establishing warmer personal relationships can we achieve the cooperation necessary to accomplish the very complex tasks facing our organizations and institutions today. Competition between individuals, groups, and nations is desired only so long as needed cooperation is not neglected—and such cooperation requires interpersonal trust.

Other scholars such as Sidney Jourard[3] argue that only by increasing our trust of one another and disclosing our thoughts and feelings can we find and maintain personal psychological health. By seeking to maintain our defenses, masks, barriers and charades, we undermine our own mental health.

We can all agree that it would be a great thing if people would trust each other more. Probably we could accomplish greater and more complex tasks; we could ease part of the strain of emotional stress and disturbance in our society. But you and I cannot make such decisions for everybody; we are stuck with the fact that we can only speak for ourselves. So the question boils down to this: *Should we be more trusting of those people around us, the ones with whom we talk and interact today?* The scholars and participants in the Human Potential Movement would say yes, do so. On a limited basis we tend to agree—it might be worth a try. But are the people we know really that trustworthy? This question assumes a pivotal position. In the long run, a general attitude of trust toward others must be based on an overall view of people—our concept of human nature.

APPROPRIATE BASES FOR A PERSONAL ETHIC

We have raised these general questions: Is it a good idea to trust people? Should we try to extend or increase our trust of others? These are questions of ethics—what is the ethical thing to do in such situations?

An ethic is a prescribed way of behaving or doing things. It states what we *ought* to do in certain situations or circumstances. For example, you probably have been told that you ought to be courteous to others, even if you can see no immediate return on such investment for you. Probably you have come to believe that we ought to extend equal rights or opportunities to black people, Chicanos, and women. Perhaps you believe that you should do unto others as you would have them do unto you.

An ethic is based on a set of human values or a value system. It involves good and bad, right and wrong, and identifies behaviors that are deserving of praise or blame. For example; most of us can agree that it is unethical (wrong) to lie, steal, tell malicious half-truths, or suggest degrading innuendos about others.

Ethics often have to do with our choices of goals—what is personally good for us in the long run. However, the means that are chosen to achieve these goals must be examined and evaluated as well as the goals themselves.

The final consideration in adoption of an ethic is the degree that it serves us in achieving life satisfaction or happiness. The golden rule—do unto others as you would have them do unto you—has been advocated by so many different races and cultures for so many centuries because, in the long run, people have found that it helps them to live satisfying lives. In determining the value of an ethic, that is, assessing its usefulness in achieving life satisfaction, two approaches are ordinarily used.

First, a purview is taken of what is ordinarily done (in a specific set of circumstances or conditions) by people who are seen as happy, satisfied, or successful in achieving a good life. This is a very practical approach for adopting an ethic; it simply asks what works or is found to be functionally satisfying to most people. In a sense, a norm of behavior is thus defined in terms of what is found to be functionally useful.

A second approach to choosing an ethic is one that is more idealistic or visionary. It is based on a view of what *could* be optimally rewarding to people even though such behavior is seldom achieved by the average person. Such an approach reaches out for the best that humankind has within its potential. Often it goes beyond that which has ever been achieved by anybody, calling for us to extend ourselves toward an idealized way of behaving. Sometimes such visions are quite unrealistic and probably unattainable. On the other hand, on many occasions in times of stress, emergency, natural disaster, or at the instigation of some charismatic visionary leader, some people have achieved that which few people have even attempted. Notable examples of

visionary systems of ethical behavior in human relations are inherent in Carl Rogers' book *On Becoming a Person*[4] and in Abraham Maslow's *The Farther Reaches of Human Nature.*[5] To a large extent the influence of these two men and their writings have spearheaded what has come to be called the Human Potential Movement. They have proclaimed an ethic involving personal growth and development—self-actualization—realizing one's own goals by achieving warmer or friendlier relations with others, achieving one's image of one's own potential by enhancing one's own self-esteem. The basic viewpoint regarding human nature is that men and women are good—benevolent and just; benevolent in the sense that they generally have goodwill toward others and prefer to try to help others achieve that which will make them happy rather than hinder these efforts; and just in the sense that they feel all persons should be treated fairly, without partiality.

Both Rogers and Maslow see people as being *in the process of developing,* not fixed or incapable of change or improvement. Individual differences are to be accepted and put to use rather than feared, defended, or resisted. Also, one's feelings are to be expressed and used for improving relationships rather than walled off. In this way interpersonal problems can be identified and possibly solved rather than stored for future irritation or explosions. Strong emphasis is placed on being yourself rather than on using masks, ploys, or games. Simple disagreement is not viewed as a difficulty leading to distrust and further difficulty; rather, disagreement is seen as having potential value in suggesting alternative ways of resolving problems. In sum, a positive approach is taken, assuming positive value outcomes from human interaction. Some risk is required, and a basic minimum of interpersonal trust is expected.

We realize, of course, that many of the ideas expressed above are not in any sense new to you. As a young adult, you have thought many times about the issues involved in such a view of human nature. Also, you have adopted your own set of ethics involving interaction with other people. As a child we were all exposed to various models of behavior and teachings about "right" ways of treating people. Early along the way we began to develop a conscience, a sense of right and wrong. As an adolescent we very likely found our experience suggesting that some of our childhood teachings were not perfect, not final; probably we found ourselves at variance with some of our earlier models or instructors. As we became aware that laws and statutes were nothing more than carefully codified statements of how we should behave, we probably realized that many of them should be reviewed and possible changes given careful consideration.

All societies have developed ethical systems, many of them similar in major essentials but different in small but significant ways.[6] For example, most societies require an apology when you accidentally bump into someone. Many of them require that you patiently await your proper turn when you join a waiting line of people. Most of them expect you to give some sort of recognition when you meet an acquaintance. However, regardless of what we were taught as children, and irrespective of how many different cultures teach courtesy in human interaction, each of us individually as adults must decide for ourselves what is right and what is wrong. On what basis can we make such a decision? What is an appropriate basis for adopting an ethic or an ethical system?

In our view both the normative approach described above, as well as the idealistic approach, have real merit. In effect, we advocate a combination of the two: looking toward the idealized optimum potential of human nature as we strive to deal with one another, but moderating our idealism by a sense of what really is achievable. In addition we suggest that we carefully note the *range* of behavior that is thought to be average or normal, and then set our interaction goals along the more optimistic end of the range of such normative behaviors.

In the long run, an appropriate basis for adoption of a value system or system of ethics is, first, what works well for an individual in terms of bringing that person a sense of life satisfaction or personal happiness.[7] This choice cannot be too deviant from what is ordinary or normal for his/her immediate social milieu; if it is too deviant, his/her friends and associates will criticize or ostracize until happiness is significantly diminished. Second, one's choice of ethics should be made on the optimistic or hopeful side of a view of human potential; by constantly seeking and striving to live up to one's best hopes or dreams, we tend to create a better world—or at least give it a chance.

When we adopt an ethic or an ethical system, in effect, we are staking a claim. Our choice can be based on what works for many people or it can incorporate what appears to us to be the highest aspirations of humanity. Even so, it is still a claim, not more, not less. An ethical claim is a proclamation of what we think people *ought* to do or be, describing what our conscience tells us is right and wrong. As a claim, we may live by it ourselves and call for other people to do the same. However, we must remember that it is *our* claim, and we must not be too surprised if other people ignore it, deny it, or interact with us according to some other ethical system of their own. Still, we can proclaim our own choice and attempt to live by it, and if successful, we may be able to show others a better way.

THE CASE FOR TRUSTING OTHERS

There are at least three good reasons for adopting an ethic that increases one's trust of others. These reasons involve consideration of interpersonal relations, one's self-image, and one's own psychological health.

In the first place, increased trust of others tends to elicit their trust of us. In this way, as we have suggested, we provide a better climate for cooperative action. In the industrial organizational world, such cooperation can help us do our jobs—work together in better fashion with less tension and fewer interpersonal problems. It can

also give us a greater sense of personal pleasure in that we can enjoy meeting and being with people.

Second, as we have shown, increasing our trust of others can improve our own self-image. In many cases, opening up ourselves to others will provide an avenue for positive feedback in return, thus validating our desired image of ourselves. Also, achieving such feedback, even if negative, can be beneficial and constructive in that we are led to see things in ourselves that need improving. In addition, we may obtain helpful suggestions on how such improvement can be made. Usually, along with such constructive suggestions, we also receive from others encouragement to try to change, stimulation to make the effort because of the potential they see in us.

The third reason for adopting an ethic of generally trusting others is that it increases our chances for psychological health. Being distrustful, defensive, anxious, scared, closed to others, avoiding interactions, all tend to increase our worries and neuroses; we tend to see images of danger in the shadows, often worrying ourselves needlessly. Some lives are lived in the shadows; some people aimlessly prowl the highways, tensely perform their jobs, slowly swallow their TV dinners, routinely quarrel, worry about their children, sigh for the unfortunate and avoid them, envy those who are happy and seek their approval, work to forget their meaningless lives, drink to forget their meaningless work, become defensive of their little "freedoms," and fret endlessly about "what has become of their lives."

The person who has learned to trust others, not just when he/she approves of them, but even at times when he/she does not, will find in trusting others a source of personal growth and self-development. This person can walk in the sun with confidence, meeting difficulties and disagreements with poise, laughing and thoroughly enjoying the good things that life has to offer. Such a person is not on the brink of mental illness; rather, he/she is in very good psychological condition.

THE DANGERS OF TRUSTING PEOPLE

As we finished rereading the previous section of this chapter, the thought came to us, why would anyone not want to trust anybody? There are good reasons why one should think twice about trusting everybody, even though the case for increasing our trust of others is a compelling one. These dangers have been discussed to some degree in previous chapters; we shall summarize them briefly here. They involve possible loss of status, damage to one's personality and self-image, deterioration of interpersonal relations with others, and possible social alienation.

In trusting others, there is a very real possibility they may use deception to our disadvantage.[8] Although our society generally condemns deception—putting something over on someone —it is frequently practiced and even loosely applauded. In some cases, people show genuine contempt for those who are "taken." Although in a general way our society holds an ethic of persuasion in which there will be no deception, only open and complete exposure of facts along with complete opportunity for one's listeners to make up their own minds unassisted and unguided, it is obvious that businessmen, salesmen, advertisers, and even teachers often violate this ethic.[9] In reality, we tend to do less than tell the truth. Telling a person the truth actually requires concern for his/her needs and purposes, consideration of his/her special and best interests. Telling the truth involves providing another person with the *necessary understanding* of a situation or condition so that he/she can make useful decisions in terms of his/her personal goals—not yours. For example, if you are walking along a campus street and a person in a car pulls over and asks you how far it is to the field house (five blocks) and you say, "It's only a little way along this same street," for this listener's observable purposes, you are telling the truth. But suppose a person in a wheel chair, or a blind person asks you the same question. You would hardly be telling the truth unless you mentioned the two steep hills along the way or the heavy cross-traffic at three intervening intersections. Telling the truth involves concern for the *needs* of the other person, and your *intentions* regarding provision of the understanding required by the other person play an important role. To a large extent our society does not demand that we tell each other the truth in this way. The old idea of "let the buyer beware" seems to hold in many of our commercial and social transactions. Because our "tell the truth" ethic is so vague, and is often violated, we run a certain chance of being deceived when we extend our trust to others. In most such cases of deception, the least that will happen is that we will suffer some loss in status or perhaps some material loss that serves as a status symbol.

A second danger in extending trust to people is the potential damage that unfulfilled trust may do to your personality or self-image. When one has been deceived again and again, by those he/she trusts, openness tends to be abandoned, defensiveness takes over, suspicion becomes habit and human interaction is diminished.[10] It is very easy for a person adopting a closed, tense,

"You know, Bill, you're the only man who can disagree with me and make me feel good about it!"

anxious way of life to conclude that something is wrong with him/her. In such a condition we tend to see how other people trust one another and don't get hurt; we may easily conclude that we are more stupid, less capable, or just less fortunate than most. In any case, there is a definite possibility that our self-image will be damaged and the interpersonal relations aspects of our personality somewhat distorted.

A third reason for being careful in extending trust to others is that our general approach to human interaction can deteriorate. Instead of seeking to satisfy our natural need to associate, we seek to avoid; instead of trying to cooperate or collaborate, we seek to gain some hold or advantage; instead of trying to enjoy being with other people, we view them with distaste, hoping to keep them from using us. Such negative orientations toward other people seem to us, as we write these lines, the start of a self-fulfilling prophecy. If we relate to others in such suspicious, distrustful ways, they are not likely to trust us. As distrust and loneliness increase, the negative expectations at the heart of such an orientation toward others will be fulfilled.

In the final analysis, a person who is in real difficulty but who is still not considered to be mentally ill is one who is severely alienated from other people. In extending your trust to others, there is this possibility: if your trust is shown to be unmerited by enough of them, and if you can obtain no explanation from them of why you were thus treated—if they deny you any opportunity to discuss with them your and their perceptions of what happened and why—there is a real chance that you will find yourself in a condition of social alienation.[11] You will tend to distrust all promises made to you by others; you will seek to avoid relying on others; you will tend to avoid inter-action, probably avoid being with people. When you must negotiate for life's essentials, you will listen only partly to what is said. You will scan the interpersonal horizon, looking for someone you can trust; but when you think you have almost found somebody, you will eventually avoid them, fearing that, once again, your trust will be used against you. This dismal picture is not the ordinary one—few people actually arrive at social alienation. Even so, some people are socially alienated, and misuse of a person's trust enough times can make it happen.

OUR VIEW ON THE ETHICS OF TRUST

The first ethic we would suggest is that we should seek to extend our trust of others. We ought to increase our trust of those around us. This is our basic ethic regarding interpersonal trust, but we will qualify it with our second one. Our reason for making this ethic basic is that it seems obvious that people should seek to enjoy themselves as their lives touch the lives of others. And it is apparent that people who succeed in trusting one another live happier, more satisfying lives.

There are many situations where human enterprise or pleasure would disappear if nobody trusted anybody. Most commercial transactions —contracts, sales, loans, and so forth—require trust of one another. Also, social arrangements— dates, games, parties, engagements and mar-riages—all require interpersonal trust to be satisfying. Most human interaction could not take place if people did not trust each other. Of course, to some extent risks are reduced by laws, credit checks, legal penalties, and public sanc-tions. Sometimes risks are also diminished by periods of engagement before marriage or persons living together before marriage. Even so, much human interaction imposes risk and re-quires trust since future acts are not entirely predictable.

To the extent that most people have taken such risks, extended personal trust, and found the results fairly satisfactory, we have established an ethical basis for extending our trust—it works most of the time for most people.

Increasing one's trust of others can provide a basis for increased collaboration with others, and collaboration in the sense of working together, playing together or just enjoying one another's company can increase our chances of achieving a happier life. We have used the word collaboration instead of cooperation because, to us, it sug-gests the idea of each person preserving his/her own sense of self-identity. We believe that colla-boration preserves respect for each other as an individual; it requires personal strength and courage.[12]

In recent years cooperation has become a good word and competition a bad word for many people. We wish to avoid both of these words. We do not wish to suggest that people should cooperate to the extent that they lose their identities; we *do* wish to suggest that competing with one another is a basic, healthy, human activity, and that, properly understood, it should not be degraded. We suggest that people should compete in the sense that any or all may be winners. Severe competition in the sense that for every winner there must be one or more losers is not good. It calls to mind the following conver-sation: "Well, after all, winning isn't everything." "Yeah, but losing isn't anything." A real loser costs everybody in the long run. In a frame of reference where there have to be losers, the winners eventually also pay a price. True col-laboration requires that interpersonal conflict be reduced, but it allows for disagreement in talking over plans for work, games, recreation, or fun. Disagreements must be resolved, but they are not viewed as crippling to the collaborative effort.

In times of technological advance and complex industrial and social arrangements, collaboration has become more necessary than ever before. This requirement imposes a real need for us to increase our ability to trust one another. Even so, collaborative effort need not require that we allow others to control us, manipulate us, or take away our freedom to work or play alone; the collabora-tive ethic requires that both you and the other person respect each other's individual potential.

We would like to suggest that in a world where much collaboration is essential, there is still room for a person to be aggressive. We use this term in the sense that a person tries to become something that he/she can respect, and achieves high self-acceptance. A person may seek to become a leader, a person whose ideas and judg-ment are respected by others. He/she probably will try to achieve high status in the eyes of his/ her peers. All of these goals can be aggressively pursued without loss of ability to collaborate as needed. Aggressive action need not necessarily be destructive. It springs from the innate tendency in all of us to grow, develop, and master life. Such a tendency seems to be characteristic of all people and most animals.

The second major ethic that we would suggest regarding interpersonal trust is one that tends to modify our first: *Our trust of others should be tentative.* We ought to offer it a little at a time; the conditions involved should be clearly specified. We should not offer it wholesale, but retail. What we are hoping to achieve by trusting another person should be made clear to that person; he/she should know what we are risking, what we are counting on them to do or be, and what we expect to achieve. We should be ready to extend and increase our trust of others, but we should be careful; we should not waste trust or foolishly throw it away. We should ask ourselves very carefully why we believe we should trust a specific other person. We should be aware of our motives and emotions. If we can understand why we feel as we do, we can better guard ourselves against throwing our trust away.

We assume that people can rationally determine what is best for them, that is, what works well in achieving their own goals and life satisfaction. However, we should be careful that we are not foolish—dupes of con men and manipulators. The proper basis for trusting another person is some assurance that such a person has a basic respect for your integrity. He/she should not want you to trust him/her unless you have reached this decision by yourself, without any persuasion on his/her part—only be your own thoughtful assessment of relevant information.

Our third ethic regarding trust is a selfish one, but in our opinion, necessary for survival: *Trust should be given, but it also should be earned.* An act of trust is unethical unless the trusted person is trustworthy—it takes two to trust one. Unless the trusted person merits your trust, you should not trust him/her very much. If your early trials of trusting prove to be undeserved, you ought not to trust a person further.

Our final goal in trusting others is *to encourage others to be trustworthy* as well as to extend our trust. In turn, we should strive to become more trustworthy ourselves and establish a proper basis for mutual trust between ourselves and others. In the long run, our goal should be collaboration with justice for all, *including ourselves.* But in so trying to achieve justice, we must always be prepared to give it. Regardless of how we are treated, we should always give only that which is just to others. Even when we are treated poorly, we should not retaliate in unjust ways; we should always give justice whether we receive it or not. In so doing, we may occasionally give better than we receive, but in this way we tend to create a better world for ourselves as well as others.

In extending and increasing our trust of others, offering it on a tentative basis, withholding it when the other person shows it is unmerited, we must learn to trust in about the same way we must learn to love—not only well, but wisely.

SUMMARY

In this chapter we have discussed the question: To what extent should you try to increase your trust of others? We have identified this question as one of ethics based upon a personal value system of what is good or bad, right or wrong.

We have raised this question and given it the emphasis of an entire chapter because of a recent cultural emphasis on extending trust of others,

influenced in part by the Human Potential Movement in our society; the development of college courses in interpersonal communication and human relations; and the need for mutual trust posed by the very complex and interdependent economic and social structure in our culture.

We have suggested that an appropriate basis for choosing one's personal ethics is a combination of (1) what works well for other people, providing them with a satisfying life, and (2) an optimistic view of humanity's greatest potential.

We have reviewed reasons suggested earlier in this book for increasing our trust of others: improved interpersonal relationships, increased self-esteem, and a better chance for achieving and maintaining personal psychological health.

We have also reviewed the potential dangers inherent in extending our trust of others: possible personal loss due to deception, potential damage to our personality through loss of self-esteem, and the possibility of eventual social alienation.

At the end of this chapter we provided our own personal view on the ethics of increasing our trust of others. We indicated that we should seek to increase our trust of people around us; this trust should be offered on a tentative basis, a small amount at a time; and our trust should be earned by those in whom we place it—it should not be needlessly wasted or thrown away.

Notes

Chapter 1

1. The concept of feedback was originally developed by Norbert Wiener, *The Human Use of Human Beings* (Boston: Houghton Mifflin, 1950). For a review of research on the concept, see J.C. Gardiner, "A Synthesis of Experimental Studies of Speech Communication Feedback," *Journal of Communication* 21 (1971): 17–35.

2. An individual's attitude toward him/herself and the world is fixed by one or two years of age and at least by age seven according to Eric Berne, *Games People Play* (New York: Grove, 1964); Erik Erikson, *Childhood and Society,* 2d ed. (New York: Norton, 1963); Gordon Allport, *Becoming* (New Haven: Yale University Press, 1964).

3. Mary S. Engel, "The Stability of the Self-Concept in Adolescence," *Journal of Abnormal and Social Psychology* 58 (1959): 211–15.

4. Thomas A. Harris, *I'm OK—You're OK* (New York: Harper and Row, 1967), credits neurosurgeon Wilder Penfield for producing evidence on memory tapes. See Wilder Penfield, "Memory Mechanisms," *A.M.A. Archives of Neurology and Psychiatry* 67 (1952): 178–98.

5. Dean C. Barnlund, "Toward a Meaning-Centered Philosophy of Communication," *Journal of Communication* 11 (1962): 198–202.

6. This issue is enunciated by many semanticists. A particularly strong argument against words reflecting a "proper meaning" is offered in I.A. Richards and C.K. Ogden, *The Meaning of Meaning* (New York: Harcourt, Brace, 1956). For a much lighter treatment of the same topic see Don Fabun, *Communications: The Transfer of Meaning* (New York: Glencoe Press, 1968).

7. W. Charles Redding, "The Organizational Communicator," *Business and Industrial Communication* (New York: Harper and Row, 1964), pp. 29–58.

8. Sidney M. Jourard and R. M. Remy, "Perceived Parental Attitudes, the Self, and Security," *Journal of Consulting Psychology* 19 (1955): 364–66.

9. Malcolm M. Helper, "Parental Evaluations of Children and Children's Self-Evaluations," *Journal of Abnormal and Social Psychology* 56 (1958): 190–94.

10. George A. Kelley, *A Theory of Personality: The Psychology of Personal Constructs* (New York: Norton, 1963).

11. Ibid., pp. 8–9.

12. A.H. Eagly, "Involvement as a Determinant of Response to Favorable and Unfavorable Information," *Journal of Personality and Social Psychology* 7 (1967): 1–15.

13. Kim Giffin, "The Contributions of Studies of Source Credibility to a Theory of Interpersonal Trust in the Communication Process," *Psychological Bulletin* 68 (1967): 104–20.

14. For a more detailed discussion of distal and proximal stimuli, see Albert Hastorf, D. Schneider and J. Polefka, *Person Perception* (Reading, Mass.: Addison-Wesley, 1970), chapter 1.

15. For example, Norman V. Peale, *A Guide to Confident Living* (New York: Prentice-Hall, 1948), and Dale Carnegie, *How to Win Friends and Influence People* (New York: Simon and Schuster, 1936).

16. Wilber Schramm, "Information Theory and Mass Communication," *Journalism Quarterly* 32 (1955): 131–46.

17. See Edward Hall, *The Silent Language* (New York: Doubleday, 1959) for an early treatment of time and space as influences upon communication.

18. Aristotle, *Rhetoric*, trans. Lane Cooper (New York: Appleton-Century-Crofts, 1932).

19. Carl I. Hovland, Irving L. Janis, and Harold H. Kelley, *Communication and Persuasion* (New Haven: Yale University Press, 1953).

20. Carl Rogers, *Client-Centered Therapy* (Boston: Houghton Mifflin, 1951).

21. Jack Gibb, "Defensive Communication," *Journal of Communication* 11 (1961): 141–48.

22. Carl Rogers, *Carl Rogers on Encounter Groups* (New York: Harper and Row, 1970), p. 10.

Chapter 2

1. Gordon W. Allport, *Personality, A Psychological Interpretation* (New York: Holt, 1937).

2. For an example of this type of exercise see Bertram B. Forer, "The Fallacy of Personal Validation: A Classroom Demonstration of Gullibility," in *Social Perception,* Hans Toch and Henry C. Smith, eds. (Princeton, N.J.: Van Nostrand, 1968).

3. *Milwaukee Journal,* March 2, 1975.

4. William M. Wiest, "A Quantitative Extension of Heider's Theory of Cognitive Balance Applied to Interpersonal Perception and Self-Esteem," *Psychological Monographs* 79, no. 14 (1965), (Whole No. 607).

5. E. Silber and Jean S. Tippett, "Self-Esteem: Clinical Assessment and Measurement Validation," *Psychological Reports* 16 (1965): 1017–71.

6. Ibid.

7. Stanley Coopersmith, *The Antecedents of Self-Esteem* (San Francisco: Freeman, 1967).

8. Donn E. Byrne, *An Introduction to Personality* (Englewood Cliffs, N.J.: Prentice-Hall, 1966).

9. See Abraham Kaplan, "The Meaning of Life to the Existentialist," *The National Observer,* November 9, 1964, p. 22, or Abraham Kaplan, *The New World of Philosophy* (New York: Vintage Books, 1961), Lecture Three.

10. Joseph Heller, *Catch-22* (New York: Dell Publishing, 1955, 1961), p. 251.

11. Richard Weaver, *The Ethics of Rhetoric* (Chicago: Henry Regnery, 1953).

12. George Kelly, *A Theory of Personality: The Psychology of Personal Constructs* (New York: Norton, 1963).

13. William Barrett, *Irrational Man* (Garden City, N.Y.: Doubleday Anchor Books, 1962).

14. Kaplan, *New World of Philosophy,* p. 98.

15. George H. Mead, *Mind, Self and Society* (Chicago: University of Chicago Press, 1934).

16. Kelly, *Theory of Personality.*

17. Barbara A. Newsom, "A Study of the Relationship of Speech Anxiety, Self-Concept, and Social Alienation" (M.A. thesis, University of Kansas, Lawrence, 1973).

18. Stanley H. Ainsworth, "A Study of Fear, Nervousness, and Anxiety in the Public Speaking Situation" (Ph.D. dissertation, Northwestern University, Evanston, Ill., 1949).

19. Gordon W. Low, "The Relationship of Psychometric Factors to Stage Fright" (unpublished M.S. thesis, University of Utah, 1950).

20. From James Bugental, *Challenges in Humanistic Psychology* (New York: McGraw-Hill, 1967), pp. 161–70.

21. The relationship between self-concept and social alienation is asserted by Ronald D. Laing, *The Self and Others* (London: Tavistoc, 1961).

22. Bernard M. Bass, et al., "Personality Variables Related to Leaderless Group Discussion Behavior," *Journal of Abnormal and Social Psychology* 48 (1953): 120–28.

23. Kim Giffin and Shirley Masterson, "A Theoretical Model of the Relationships Between Motivation and Self-Confidence in Communication," in *Communication-Spectrum '7,* Lee Thayer, ed. (Flint, Mich.:

National Society for Study of Communication, 1968), pp. 311–16.

24. John W. Atkinson and Norman T. Feather, eds., *A Theory of Achievement Motivation* (New York: Wiley, 1966).

Chapter 3

1. According to William V. Haney, *Communication and Organizational Behavior Text and Cases,* rev. ed. (Homewood, Ill.: Irwin, 1967), the eye can handle about five million bits of stimuli per second, but the brain is limited to approximately five hundred bits per second.

2. E. Lakin Phillips reported a positive correlation between a subject's perception and attitudes toward others nearly twenty-five years ago. See "Attitudes toward Self and Others: A Brief Questionnaire Report," *Journal of Consulting Psychology* 15 (1951): 79–82.

3. Hans H. Toch and Richard Schulte, "Readiness to Perceive Violence as a Result of Police Training," in *Social Perception: The Development of Interpersonal Impressions,* Hans Toch and Henry C. Smith, eds., © 1968. Reprinted by permission of D. Van Nostrand Company.

4. Ibid., p. 157.

5. Janis H. Weiss, "Effect of Professional Training and Amount of Accuracy of Information on Behavioral Prediction," *The Journal of Consulting Psychology* 27 (1963): 257–62.

6. Morton Deutsch, "Trust and Suspicion," *Journal of Conflict Resolution* 2 (1958): 265–79.

7. Carl R. Rogers, *Client-Centered Therapy* (Boston: Houghton Mifflin, 1951).

8. Elizabeth T. Sheerer, "The Relationship Between Acceptance of Self and Acceptance of Others," *Journal of Consulting Psychology* 13 (1949): 169–76.

9. Dorothy Stock, "The Self-Concept and Feelings toward Others," *Journal of Consulting Psychology* 13 (1949): 176–81.

10. Emanuel M. Berger, "The Relation between Expressed Acceptance of Self and Expressed Acceptance of Others," *Journal of Abnormal Social Psychology* 13 (1949): 176–81.

11. Charles J. McIntyre, "Acceptance by Others and Its Relation to Acceptance of Self and Others," *Journal of Abnormal Social Psychology* 47 (1952): 624–26.

12. William F. Fey, "Acceptance of Self and Others and Its Relation to Therapy-Readiness," *Journal of Clinical Psychology* 10 (1954): 269–71.

13. Robert L. Bohlken, "A Descriptive Study of the Relationship between the Communication Variable of Interpersonal Trust and Speech Teacher Effectiveness at the College Level" (Ph.D. dissertation, University of Kansas, Lawrence, 1969).

14. These results are similar to the earlier findings of Morton Deutsch, "Trust, Trustworthiness, and the F. Scale," *Journal of Abnormal and Social Psychology* 61 (1960): 138–40. Subjects who were more trusting were more likely to be trusted.

15. William M. Wiest, "A Quantitative Extension of Heider's Theory of Cognitive Balance Applied to Interpersonal Perception and Self-Esteem," *Psychological Monographs* 79, no. 14 (1965), (Whole No. 607).

16. Bernard Chodorkoff, "Self-Perception, Perceptual Defense, and Adjustment," *Journal of Abnormal Social Psychology* 49 (1954): 508–12.

17. Ralph White and Ronald Lippitt, "Leader Behavior and Member Reaction in Three 'Social Climates'," in *Group Dynamics,* Dorwin Cartwright and Alvin Zander, eds. (New York: Harper and Row, 1968), pp. 318–35.

18. Carl R. Rogers, *On Becoming a Person* (Boston: Houghton Mifflin, 1961), pp. 41–49.

19. Alfred L. Baldwin, J. Kalhorn, and F.H. Breeze, "Patterns of Parent Behavior," *Psychological Monographs* 58, no. 268 (1945): 1–75.

20. Rogers, *On Becoming a Person,* p. 56.

21. Dana Bramel, "Dissonance, Expectation, and the Self," in *Theories of Cognitive Consistency: A Sourcebook,* Robert P. Abelson et al., eds. (Chicago: Rand McNally, 1968), pp. 355–65.

22. See for example Morton Deutsch and Leonard F. Solomon, "Reactions to Evaluations by Others as Influenced by Self-Evaluations," *Sociometry* 22 (1959): 93–112.

23. William D. Brooks and Sarah M. Platz, "The Effects of Speech Training upon Self-Concept as a Communicator," *Speech Teacher* 17 (1968): 44–49, found three-fourths of those enrolled in a basic speech class improved significantly in self-concept as a communicator.

24. See Paul F. Secord, "Consistency Theory and Self-Referent Behavior," in *Theories of Cognitive Consistency: A Sourcebook,* Robert P. Abelson et al., eds. (Chicago: Rand McNally, 1968), and Martin L. Maehr, J. Mensign, and S. Nafzgher, "Concept of Self and the Reactions of Others," *Sociometry* 25 (1962): 353–57.

25. George C. Homans, "Social Behavior as Exchange," in *Current Perspectives in Social Psychology,* Edwin P. Hollander and Raymond G. Hunt, eds. (New York: Oxford University Press, 1963), pp. 436–447.

26. This practice has been advocated by many leading educators. A particularly strong case has been built by William Glasser, *Schools without Failure* (New York: Harper and Row, 1969).

27. Ernest G. Bormann and George L. Shapiro, "Perceived Confidence as a Function of Self-Image," *Central States Speech Journal* 13 (1962): 253–56.

28. Martin Buber, *I and Thou,* trans. Walter Kaufmann (New York: Scribners, 1970).

29. Paul Pfeutze, *Self, Society, Existence* (New York: Harper and Row, 1954).

30. Ibid.

Chapter 4

1. Kim Giffin and Bobby R. Patton, *Fundamentals of Interpersonal Communication* (New York: Harper and Row, 1971), pp. 18–55.

2. Karen Horney, *Our Inner Conflicts* (New York: Norton, 1945).

3. Ralph Ellison, *Invisible Man* (New York: Random House, 1952).

4. Fyodor Dostoyevsky, "Notes from Underground," in *Dostoyevsky: Notes from Underground, White Nights, The Dream of a Ridiculus Man and Selections from The House of the Dead,* Andrew R. MacAndrew, trans. (New York: New American Library, 1961), pp. 90–203.

5. Ibid., p. 129.

6. Ibid.

7. An interesting teaching guide illustrating this point has been developed by William R. Bauman, University of Kansas, "Will the Real Charles Joseph Whitman Please Stand Up."

8. "Under the Clock, A Sniper with 31 Minutes to live," *Life,* 12 August 1966, pp. 24–31.

9. Harry Chapin, "The Sniper", © Story Songs, Ltd. (ASCAP). Used by permission. All rights reserved.

10. See, for example, Thomas A. Harris, *I'm OK—You're OK* (New York: Avon, 1969).

11. Kim Giffin and Mary Heider, "A Theory of the Relationship between Adult Speech Anxiety and Suppression of Communication in Childhood," *Psychiatric Quarterly Supplement* 2 (1967): 311–22.

12. George H. Mead, *Mind, Self and Society,* ed. Charles W. Morris (Chicago: University of Chicago Press, 1934).

13. Herbert Blumer, *Symbolic Interactionism: Perspective and Method* (Englewood Cliffs, N.J.: Prentice-Hall, 1969).

14. George Mellinger, "Interpersonal Trust as a Factor in Communications," *Journal of Abnormal and Social Psychology* 52 (1956): 304–9.

15. Ibid.

16. Harold H. Kelley, "Communication in Experimentally Created Hierarchies," *Human Relations* 4 (1951): 39–56.

17. This same idea is enunciated by Anatol Rapoport, "Game Theory and Human Conflict," in *The Nature of Human Conflict,* Elton B. McNeil, ed. (Englewood Ciffs, N.J.: Prentice-Hall, 1965), p. 202.

18. J. Rotter, "A New Scale for the Measurement of Interpersonal Trust," *Journal of Personality* 35 (1967): 651–65.

19. J. Loomis, "Communication, the Development of Trust, and Cooperative Behavior," *Human Relations* 12 (1959): 305–16.

20. R. Swinth, "The Establishment of the Trust Relationship," *Journal of Conflict Resolution* 11 (1967): 335–44.

21. Morton Deutsch and R.M. Krauss, "Studies of Interpersonal Bargaining," *Journal of Conflict Resolution* 6 (1962): 52–76.

22. Harold H. Kelley, et al., "The Development of Cooperation in the 'Minimal Social Situation'," *Psychological Monograph* 76 (1962): 19.

23. Morton Deutsch, "Cooperation and Trust: Some Theoretical Notes," in *Nebraska Symposium on Motivation,* M.R. Jones, ed. (Lincoln: University of Nebraska Press, 1962), pp. 279–319.

24. Paul F. Secord and Carl W. Backman, *Social Psychology,* 2d ed. (New York: McGraw-Hill, 1966), p. 271.

25. For a general review of these studies see L.P. Ullman and L. Krasner, eds., *Case Studies in Behavior Modification* (New York: Holt, Rinehart and Winston, 1965).

26. O. Kondas, "Reduction of Examination Anxiety and 'Stage Fright' by Group Desensitization and Relaxation," *Behavior Research and Therapy* 5 (1967): 275–81.

27. Jack Gibb, "Defensive Communication," *Journal of Communication* 11 (1961): 141–48.

28. Carl Rogers, *On Becoming a Person* (New York: Houghton Mifflin, 1961).

Chapter 5

1. Solomon Asch, "Forming Impressions of Personality," *Journal of Abnormal and Social Psychology* 41 (1946): 258–90 (quotation taken from p. 258).

2. Cecil Gibb, "The Sociometry of Leadership in Temporary Groups," *Sociometry* 13 (1950): 226–43.

3. For discussion of this phenomenon and its effects see Bernard Weiner et al. "Perceiving the Causes of Success and Failure," in *Attribution: Perceiving the Causes of Behavior,* Edward E. Jones et al., eds. (Morristown, N.J.: General Learning Press, 1971), pp. 95–120.

4. Norman L. Munn, *Psychology: The Fundamentals of Human Adjustment* (Boston: Houghton Mifflin, 1947), p. 327.

5. Cf. Renato Tagiuri, "Person Perception," in *The Handbook of Social Psychology,* Gardner Lindzey and Elliot Aronson, eds., 2d ed. (Reading, Mass.: Addison-Wesley, 1969), 3:395–449; see especially pp. 418–20.

6. For a review of research on consistency theory see Marvin E. Shaw and Philip R. Costanzo, *Theories of Social Psychology* (New York: McGraw Hill, 1970), pp. 171–218.

7. Leon Festinger, *A Theory of Cognitive Dissonance* (Stanford: Stanford University Press, 1957), pp. 123–76.

8. Elliot Aronson, "Dissonance Theory: Progress and Problems," in *Source Book on Cognitive Consistency,* Robert P. Abelson et al., eds. (Chicago: Rand McNally, 1968), pp. 5–77.

9. Jonathon L. Freedman and David O. Sears, "Selective Exposure," in *Advances in Experimental Social Psychology,* Leonard Berkowitz, ed. (New York: Academic Press, 1965), 2: 57–97.

10. Norman H. Anderson, "Application of a Linear-Serial Model to a Personality-Impression Task Using Serial Presentation," *Journal of Personality and Social Psychology* 10 (1968): 354–62.

11. Robert A. Baron, Donn Byrne, and William Griffitt, *Social Psychology* (Boston: Allyn and Bacon, 1974), pp. 190–95.

12. Donn Byrne, *The Attraction Paradigm* (New York: Academic Press, 1971), pp. 127–34.

13. K.K. Dion, Ellen Berscheid and Elaine Walster, "What Is Beautiful Is Good," *Journal of Personality and Social Psychology* 24 (1972): 285–90.

14. Elaine Walster et al., "Importance of Physical Attractiveness on Dating Behavior," *Journal of Personality and Social Psychology* 4 (1968): 508–16.

15. Donn Byrne, C.R. Ervin and J. Lamberth, "Continuity between the Experimental Study of Attraction and Real-Life Computer Dating," *Journal of Personality* 36 (1968): 259–71.

16. Carl I. Hovland, Irving L. Janis, and Harold H. Kelley, *Communication and Persuasion* (New Haven: Yale University Press, 1953), p. 21.

17. Ibid., p. 35.

18. For a review of these studies see Kim Giffin, "The Contribution of Studies of Source Credibility to a Theory of Interpersonal Trust in the Communication Process," *Psychological Bulletin* 68 (1967): 104–20.

19. Kenneth E. Anderson, *Persuasion: Theory and Practice* (Boston: Allyn and Bacon, 1971), pp. 221–22. Also see Kenneth E. Anderson, "An Experimental Study of the Interaction of Artistic and Non-artistic Ethos in Persuasion" (Doctoral Dissertation, University of Wisconsin, Madison, 1961).

20. David K. Berlo, James B. Lemert, and Robert J. Mertz, "Dimensions for Evaluating the Acceptability of Message Sources," *Public Opinion Quarterly* 33 (Winter 1969–1970): 562–576.

21. James C. McCroskey, "Scales for the Measurement of Ethos," *Speech Monographs* 30 (1966): 65–72.

22. Don Schweitzer and Gerald P. Ginsburg, "Factors of Communication Credibility," in *Problems in Social Psychology,* Carl W. Backman and Paul F. Secord, eds. (New York: McGraw-Hill, 1966), pp. 94–102.

23. Ibid., p. 98.

24. Kim Giffin, *An Experimental Evaluation of the Trust Differential* (Lawrence, Kansas: The Communication Research Center, The University of Kansas, 1968).

25. See Kim Giffin, "Interaction Variables of Interpersonal Trust," *Humanitas* 9 (1973): 297–315.

26. Cf. Kim Giffin, "Interpersonal Trust in Small-Group Communication," *The Quarterly Journal of Speech* 53 (1967): 224–34.

27. Cf. Kim Giffin and Bobby R. Patton, "Personal Trust in Human Interaction," in *Basic Readings in Interpersonal Communication,* Kim Giffin and Bobby R. Patton, eds. (New York: Harper and Row, 1971), pp. 375–91.

28. Cf. Kim Giffin, "The Measurement of Interpersonal Trust," in *Research Designs in General Semantics,* Kenneth G. Johnson, ed. (New York: Gordon and Breach, 1974), pp. 89–94.

29. Cf. Kim Giffin, "The Contribution of Studies of Source Credibility to a Theory of Interpersonal Trust in the Communication Process," *Psychological Bulletin* 68 (1967): 104–20 (see especially p. 118).

30. Harold H. Kelley, "Attribution in Social Interaction," in *Attribution,* Edward E. Jones et al., eds. (Morristown, N.J.: General Learning Press, 1971), pp. 1–26.

31. Cf. Baron, Byrne, and Griffitt, *Social Psychology,* pp. 340–62.

32. Edward E. Jones and Keith E. Davis "From Acts to Dispositions: The Attribution Process in Person Perception," in *Advances in Experimental Social Psychology,* Leonard E. Berkowitz, ed. (New York: Academic Press, 1965), 2: 219–66.

33. Cf. Baron, Byrne, and Griffitt, *Social Psychology,* pp. 343–44.

34. Harold H. Kelley, "Attribution Theory in Social Psychology," in *Nebraska Symposium on Motivation,* David Levine, ed. (Lincoln: University of Nebraska Press, 1967), pp. 192–238.

35. Cf. Leslie A. McArthur, "The How and What of Why: Some Determinants and Consequences of Causal Attribution" (Ph.D. dissertation, Yale University, 1970).

36. Elaine Walster, "Assignment of Responsibility for an Accident," *Journal of Personality and Social Psychology* 3 (1966): 73–79.

37. See Edward E. Jones and Victor A. Harris, "The Attribution of Attitudes," *Journal of Experimental Social Psychology* 3 (1967): 1–24.

38. Baron, Byrne, Griffitt, *Social Psychology,* pp. 354–55.

39. Elaine Walster, Elliot Aronson, and Darcy Abrahams, "On Increasing the Persuasiveness of a New

Prestige Communicator," *Journal of Experimental Social Psychology* (1966): 325–42.

40. For a summary of research on this problem see Baron, Byrne, and Griffitt, *Social Psychology,* pp. 350–53.

41. Ibid., p. 351.

42. Ibid., p. 352.

43. For a review of exploratory research on openness see Kim Giffin and Bobby R. Patton, *Personal Communication in Human Relations* (Columbus, O.: Charles E. Merrill, 1974), pp. 12–19.

Chapter 6

1. Cf. J. Edward Hulett, Jr., "A Symbolic Interactionist Model of Human Communication," *Audio-Visual Communication Review* 14 (1966): 5–33 (see especially pp. 17–18).

2. For a detailed analysis of the major factors involved in an interpersonal relationship see Kim Giffin and Bobby R. Patton, *Personal Communication in Human Relations* (Columbus, O.: Charles E. Merrill, 1974), pp. 53–72.

3. Theodore R. Sarbin and Donald S. Jones, "An Experimental Analysis of Role Behavior," *Journal of Abnormal and Social Psychology* 52 (1955): 236–41.

4. Cf. Hulett, "Symbolic Interactionist Model," p. 17.

5. Cf. Morton Deutsch, "The Effect of Motivational Orientation upon Trust and Suspicion," *Human Relations* 13 (1960): 123–40.

6. Morton Deutsch, "Trust and Suspicion," *Journal of Conflict Resolution* 2 (1958): 265–79.

7. Deutsch, "Effect of Motivational Orientation," p. 132.

8. Ibid., pp. 132–35.

9. Leonard Solomon, "The Influence of Some Types of Power Relationships and Game Strategies upon the Development of Interpersonal Trust," *Journal of Abnormal and Social Psychology* 61 (1960): 223–30.

10. S.S. Komorita and John Mechling, "Betrayal and Reconciliation in a Two-Person Game," *Journal of Personality and Social Psychology* 6 (1967): 349–53.

11. Ibid., p. 353.

12. Solomon, "Influence of Some Types of Power Relationships," pp. 224–26.

13. For a detailed discussion of this problem along with the general problem of conceptualizing trust and trusting behavior, see W. Barnett Pearce, "Trust in Interpersonal Communication," *Speech Monographs* 41 (1974): 236–44.

14. Gary Evans, "Effect of Unilateral Promise and Value of Rewards upon Cooperation and Trust," *Journal of Abnormal and Social Psychology* 69 (1964): 587–90.

15. Ibid., p. 590.

16. Arie W. Kruglanski, "Attributing Trustworthiness in Supervisor-Worker Relations," *Journal of Experimental Social Psychology* 6 (1970): 214–32.

17. Dale G. Leathers, "The Process Effects of Trust-Destroying Behavior in the Small Group," *Speech Monographs* 37 (1970): 180–87.

18. For a detailed review of these studies and their relevance to interpersonal trust, see Kim Giffin, "Interpersonal Trust in Small-Group Communication," *The Quarterly Journal of Speech* 53 (1967): 228–33.

19. For an experimental study specifically designed to investigate this principle see Stewart L. Tubbs, "The Influence of Majority Opinion and Game Playing Behavior on Interpersonal Trust" (Ph.D. dissertation, University of Kansas, 1969). Also see Stewart L. Tubbs, "Two-Person Game Behavior, Conformity Inducing Messages, and Interpersonal Trust," *Journal of Communication* 21 (1971): 326–41.

20. Evans, "Effect of Unilateral Promise," p. 590.

21. James N. Farr, "The Effects of a Disliked Third Person upon the Development of Mutual Trust" (Paper presented to the American Psychological Association Annual Conference, New York, September 1957).

Chapter 7

1. See, for example, Jack R. Gibb, "Climate for Trust Formation," in *T-Group Theory and Laboratory Method,* Leland P. Bradford, Jack R. Gibb, and Kenneth D. Benne, eds. (New York: Wiley, 1964), pp. 279–309.

2. See, for example, Rensis Likert, *The Human Organization* (New York: McGraw-Hill, 1967).

3. See Sidney Jourard, *Disclosing Man to Himself* (Princeton, N.J.: Van Nostrand, 1968).

4. Carl Rogers, *On Becoming a Person* (Boston: Houghton Mifflin, 1961).

5. Abraham H. Maslow, *The Farther Reaches of Human Nature* (New York: Viking, 1971).

6. For a fairly complete discussion of the ethics of interaction, see Thomas R. Nilson, *Ethics of Speech Communication* (New York: Bobbs-Merrill, 1966).

7. See, for example, the philosophical arguments presented by Paul W. Keller and Charles T. Brown, "An Interpersonal Ethic for Communication," *Journal of Communication* 18 (1968): 73–81.

8. For a very interesting treatment of the concept of deception in human communication see Mark L. Knapp, Roderick P. Hart, and Harry S. Dennis, "An Exploration of Deception as a Communication Construct," *Human Communication Research* 1 (1974): 15–29.

9. For a fairly complete discussion of deception in our culture see Ben Bursten, *The Manipulator* (New Haven: Yale University Press, 1973), pp. 1–23.

10. Cf. Kim Giffin and Bobby R. Patton, *Fundamentals of Interpersonal Communication* (New York: Harper and Row, 1971), pp. 18–40.

11. Cf. Kim Giffin, "Social Alienation by Communication Denial," *Quarterly Journal of Speech* 56 (1970): 347–58.

12. For an extensive treatment of the collaborative process to which we refer see Bobby R. Patton and Kim Giffin, *Problem Solving Group Interaction* (New York: Harper and Row, 1973).

Index